Red Star Over Cuba

RED STAR
OVER CUBA

THE RUSSIAN ASSAULT
ON THE WESTERN HEMISPHERE

Nathaniel Weyl

THE DEVIN-ADAIR COMPANY, *Publishers*
New York
1960

Contents

Introduction: The Guilty and the Deluded

> "However, the present writer believes that the 'Bogotazo' as most Latin Americans call these events, was in no way the work of the Communists."
>
> —Robert J. Alexander
> *Communism in Latin America*[1]

THE Bogotá uprising of 1948, or "Bogotazo," was the first massive demonstration of Red military and political power in the Western Hemisphere. It was directed chiefly against the United States. Its primary purposes were: to force the Ninth Inter-American Conference, then meeting at Bogotá, to close its doors and to force the delegates to that conference to flee for their lives; to overthrow the democratically elected government of Colombia and substitute a leftist regime responsible to the armed mob; probably, but not certainly, to engineer the assassination of the U. S. Secretary of State, General of the Armies George C. Marshall.

[1] Rutgers University Press, New Brunswick, N. J., 1957, p. 250. Dr. Alexander's book has importance because it is used for indoctrination of Foreign Service personnel by the Department of State.

That the Bogotazo was a Communist operation was the conclusion of General Marshall, of C.I.A. director Admiral Hillenkoetter, of U.S. Ambassador to Colombia Willard L. Beaulac, of the President of Colombia Dr. Mariano Ospina Pérez, of the brilliant and scholarly General Secretary of the Presidency of the Colombian Republic, Rafael Azula Barrera, and of other responsible eyewitnesses and analysts of these tragic events.

At this juncture, I shall cite merely one or two of these witnesses. "Secretary of State George C. Marshall, president of the American delegation, was the especial target of Communist lies and insults," United States Ambassador Beaulac wrote in his memoirs. "It was freely and apparently reliably reported that the Communists planned to demonstrate against the conference and, if possible, to cause riots and even civil war in an effort to break it up."[2] The independent Colombian newspaperman, Francisco Fandiño Silva, recalled, "The American Embassy advised me that it had received reports that a bomb attack was to be made against the eminent General (Marshall)."[3] Yet, between January and March 1948, the detailed and highly competent C.I.A. reports on Soviet preparations for insurrectionary action were not forwarded to Secretary of State Marshall as they should have been, but were blocked in the American Embassy at Bogotá.[4]

---

[2] Willard L. Beaulac, *Career Ambassador*, Macmillan, New York, 1951, p. 236.

[3] Francisco Fandiño Silva, *La penetración Soviética en América y el 9 de abril*, Colección "Nuevos Tiempos," Bogotá, 1949.

[4] These C.I.A. reports were released in part to a Congressional committee of inquiry after the holocaust by Admiral Hillenkoetter and published in the press.

The Senate Internal Security Subcommittee had this to say about the pigeonholing of these reports:

"The reaction of the representatives of the United States to these timely warnings was typical of our official disregard and contempt for the power of Communist mass agitation. O. J. Libert, State Department aide in Bogotá and Ambassador Willard L. Beaulac were charged by Admiral Hillenkoetter with failure to forward these messages to the State Department in Washington. Mr. Libert vetoed sending these messages to Secretary Marshall's security

There is ample and voluminous documentation on the Bogotá uprising. Despite this, Fidel Castro's sinister role in these events has been ignored, sugarcoated or misrepresented by his eulogistic American biographers and by partisan foreign correspondents. Efforts have been made to explain Castro's conduct as some sort of youthful lark. It was nothing of the sort.

Had American officials and publicists made a diligent and serious study of the role of Fidel Castro in the Bogotá uprising, they could scarcely have escaped the conclusion that, as early as 1948, he was not merely an implacable enemy of the United States, but a trusted Soviet agent as well. In the case of at least one foreign correspondent, sympathy for Communism and Communist causes seems to have been a motivating reason for a consistent failure to report the facts with anything approximating objectivity.

The failure to identify the Fidel Castro movement in its incipient stages as Communist, helped bring oppression and terror to the Cuban people and contributed to weakening the power, prestige and security of the United States in this Hemisphere.

In the chapters that follow, I shall try to show that the clues to the character of Fidel Castro and his insurgent movement were clear at all times to those having eyes to see with and brains to reason with; that the development of the 26th of July movement assumed the fairly conventional pattern of a Communist cover operation; that the State

---

officers because he thought Bogotá police protection 'adequate,' and he did not wish to 'alarm the delegates unduly.' Former Secretary of State George C. Marshall was quoted by the State Department press officer, Lincoln White, as saying in the course of some 'salty remarks' that it was 'quite ridiculous to suppose that the 21 American Republics should even consider being intimidated by the protestations of one kind or another from Communists, or from anybody else.'

"Meanwhile, the Communists simply waited for the most propitious moment to strike." Senate Internal Security Subcommittee, *Communist Threat to the United States Through the Caribbean*, Hearings, Part II, August 13, 1959, Appendix, "Communist Anti-American Riots—Mob Violence as an Instrument of Red Diplomacy" (staff report), p. 116.

Department was repeatedly warned of the Communist character of this movement, but chose to disregard such warnings; and that, once their movement triumphed, Fidel Castro and his associates followed standard Sino-Soviet operating procedures for the seizure and consolidation of power.

There are honest and reasonably competent observers of the Cuban scene who assume that Fidel Castro is an hysteric, a paranoid personality, a cyclothyme, a psychopath, an epileptic or a drug addict, or that he suffers from some other form of mental illness. They infer from this that he cannot be taken seriously as a Communist leader and that the "true Communists" are doubtless lurking in the background, waiting for the mountebank to fall off the stage, at which point they will themselves take power and wield it in an even more sinister manner.

This approach rests on false or misleading assumptions and leads to self-defeating policies. If one assumes that Fidel Castro is a mentally disturbed and irresponsible demagogue, who is manipulated in evil directions by his Communist advisers, then it can be argued that American policy should seek to drive a wedge between the dictator and those closest to him and that, to that extent, it should be a policy of appeasement.

However, the evidence, as I shall show, reveals Fidel Castro to be a seasoned and highly competent Soviet agent. As for the many journalistic diagnoses of his mental condition, some are mutually incompatible and others are based on fragmentary evidence. It is probable, however, that Castro has a psychopathic personality.

The more important point is that mental illness does not necessarily prevent a man from being an efficient and ruthless dictator, a crafty politician and the incarnation of a secular ideology or religious creed. Adolf Hitler could scarcely have been described as a normal man. There is a good deal of evidence that Stalin, in his later years, suffered from a progressive paranoid condition. André Marty was one of the chief leaders of the French Communist Party for thirty years despite the fact that he was a moral monster, a sadist and the victim of delusions of persecution.[5]

The political stature of Fidel Castro can be judged very simply—by looking at what he has accomplished. Using brilliant public relations techniques, he managed to parlay an insignificant guerrilla operation (which had at its nadir a total effective strength of about 15 men) into a movement which made the front pages of the world's press and which eventually seized power in Cuba. By means of interminable harangues and the lavish use of radio and television, he made himself the greatest individual force in Cuba within months after the seizure of power, in the sense that his features, his voice, his prejudices and his opinions were indelibly burned into the minds of millions of people, many of whom had previously been apolitical. He successfully deceived the American government and the American people as to his true character and purposes long enough to create a mass movement, a so-called people's militia and the usual apparata of espionage and terror, all fanatically loyal to him and to his Communist program. He managed to insult the United States again and again with impunity. Within the time-span of less than two years, the dictator of a tropical island of minor economic importance, inhabited by only 7 million people, succeeded in making himself one of the best known political leaders in the world.

These achievements are sufficiently impressive to make it quite impossible to dismiss Fidel Castro as unstable, insane, a figurehead or a mere demagogue. When we do this, we merely reveal our own insularity and parochialism. Worse, we show a basic ignorance of the world in which we live. The fact that a political ruler has atrocious table manners, that he is careless about washing, that he functions in a disor-

[5] Survivors of the Spanish Civil War have told me that Ernest Hemingway's portrayal of Marty in the closing chapters of *For Whom the Bell Tolls* is entirely accurate.

ganized and chaotic fashion, that he seldom reasons clearly or consecutively about anything, that he indulges in trance-like harangues and that he incessantly evokes the resentment, hatred and cruelty of a mass which lacks comfort or privilege—all this is no reason to discount him. For it is almost exclusively in the prosperous and educated republics of the West that reason prevails, and at that only partially, in politics, whereas in other, less fortunate areas, the demagogue, the terrorist and, for that matter, the psychopath seem increasingly prone to emerge as the masters of their nations.

NATHANIEL WEYL

Cadaqués
Spain
September 24, 1960

1

The Bogotá Uprising

> "You must know, then, that
> there are two methods of
> fighting, the one by law,
> the other by force: the first
> method is that of men, the
> second of beasts; but as the
> first method is often insuffi-
> cient, one must have re-
> course to the second."
> —Niccolò Machiavelli
> *The Prince*[1]

THE Bogotá uprising of 1948 was the arena in
which Fidel Castro played his first serious role as an instiga-
tor and organizer of Communist insurrection. At the time, he
was 21 years old and a student in the faculty of laws of Havana University. He had been exposed to Communist indoctrination for the past two years, had accepted Marxian
ideology eagerly and had probably submitted himself to Communist discipline. On this last point, there is some difference
of opinion.

While he was disliked, rejected or regarded with indiffer-
ence by the majority of the student body, Fidel Castro was
a leader among the highly politicalized revolutionary ele-

---

[1] Modern Library edition, New York, 1940, p. 64. Translation by Luigi Ricci,
revised by E. R. P. Vincent.

ment addicted to violence and terrorism. He had acquired military training and proved his resourcefulness in the Cayo Confites expedition which had prepared the invasion of the Dominican Republic the previous year. He had personally participated in an attempted murder—the ambushing and gunning down of Léonel Gomez, a high school student whom he regarded as a political rival, and he had been arrested for two political murders of a similar character, in which the student victims were machinegunned in the streets of Havana at night in Chicago gangster style.

Fidel Castro had done practically no studying at the University and had acquired very little learning. He had however, acquired a police dossier, in which he was described as a terrorist and criminal element. The dossier stated categorically that he had committed the two murders referred to in the previous paragraph.

Castro, at the time, was a man of immense drive and magnetism. Partly due to his illegitimacy, he was without strong social roots, suspended between classes, a member of the upper classes by reason of wealth, appearance and intelligence, but in chronic rebellion because he was never completely accepted. His ambitions were limitless, probably because his sense of insecurity made it psychically necessary that he prove his own superiority. His experiences in homicide were of significance because they reinforced psychopathic elements in his character structure. He would act without any moral restraints, kill or organize killings when it suited his political purposes, and make power and expediency the sole criteria of his conduct.

In addition to his dynamic qualities as a revolutionary leader, Castro had the enormous advantage of not being labeled as a Communist. This made him much more useful to the Soviet and Communist forces engaged in preparing the Bogotá blood bath than if he had been so branded. Fidel Castro's youth was, of course, an unfavorable factor, but by no means an insuperable one. International Communism had learned to promote promising men to positions of high responsibility regardless of age. In the Latin American scene, Rómulo Betancourt had become the leader of the Costa Rican Communist Party at the age of 22; Julio Antonio Mella became General Secretary of the Mexican Party in his mid-20's; Ricardo Martinez was named Latin American representative to the Profintern before the age of 30.

The Gathering Storm

On June 5, 1947, in a speech delivered at Harvard, Secretary of State George C. Marshall announced an American plan for the economic rehabilitation of Europe. The Marshall Plan, as it would soon be called, was designed to bring about rapid European recovery so that the continent could eliminate the ever-present threat of chaos and provide firm economic foundations for free institutions. This plan was one of several major American steps to build a rampart against Soviet infiltration or invasion of western and central Europe. It was so interpreted by the Soviet Government. Accordingly, the Communist Parties of the world took an increasingly sharp anti-American position.

The effort to shatter the Ninth Inter-American Conference at Bogotá, to topple the Conservative government of the country serving as host to that conference and to provide visual demonstration of the power of the armed Communist-led mob to spread havoc and death was part of this general anti-United States strategy.

A second major focus of conspiracy was Rómulo Betancourt. As a young man, Betancourt had been expelled from his native Venezuela for radical agitation. Proceeding to Costa Rica, he had been the leader of the Communist Party during 1930-35. He resigned from the Party, primarily because he thought its methods were stupid, returned to Venezuela and organized the Democratic Action Party which was socialist and far to the left, but which claimed to have no Communist links.[2] In 1945, he took advantage of the discontent of young Venezuelan army officers to overthrow the government and take power as leader of a revolutionary junta. In December 1947, elections were held and Democratic Action rolled up a large majority. The leftwing novelist, Rómulo Gallegos, was installed as President of Venezuela, leaving Betancourt free to busy himself with Caribbean intrigues.[3]

Betancourt invited Jorge Eliecer Gaitán, the leader of the Colombian Liberal Party who would later be assassinated, to Caracas for conversations. In these earnest discussions, Betancourt apparently tried to persuade Gaitán to resort to armed insurrection, but failed. As the Venezuelan Catholic Youth and National Anti-Communist Youth put the matter in a joint report:

"The Liberal leader, Jorge Eliecer Gaitán, used to tell friends how Betancourt had offered him arms and money to launch a revolution in Colombia, and to take over power along the lines of his ideas of a popular world-wide revolution. Gaitán consistently refused the Betancourt proposals and continued his personal crusade against both extreme Left and Right—as well as feuding with his own Liberal Party. So he was murdered." [4]

Betancourt's apparent purpose was to build a solid phalanx of leftwing regimes in the Caribbean, both to enhance

[2] In a 1931 pamphlet entitled *The Minimum Program of Penetration,* Betancourt foreshadowed his later approach to revolutionary strategy and tactics. He wrote:

"We can introduce Lenin and Stalin to these (Latin American) people by using vaseline. We can build up a passionate hatred of private property and a vital and active determination to get rid of the capitalist system. We can do all this without using that word which reeks of sulphur and brimstone, Communism."

[3] Here and elsewhere, I deal with Rómulo Betancourt's cooperation with the forces of international Communism, his schemes to subvert the constitutional government of Colombia and his complicity in the attempted wrecking of the Ninth Inter-American Conference. Needless to say, these events occurred in 1948 and do not necessarily reflect Betancourt's policies and purposes in 1960.

[4] Venezuelan Catholic Youth and National Anti-Communist Front, October 1958.

the power of his revolutionary organization and to protect the leftwing regime in Venezuela against being overthrown.[5] In this, Betancourt could count on the support of the Caribbean Legion, the non-Communist leftwing governments of Figueres in Costa Rica and Prío Socarrás in Cuba, the Communist-influenced regime of Arévalo in Guatemala and the Soviet-dominated Latin American Labor Federation (CTAL) of Lombardo Toledano.[6]

Revolution in Colombia suited the purposes of Betancourt and of international Communism, but not those of Dr. Gaitán. In the previous Colombian national elections of May 1946, the Liberal Party of Colombia had been split into two factions and, hence, had lost. Since then, the leader of the more moderate Liberal group had died, leaving Gaitán undisputed master of the strongest political party in Colombia. Gaitán not only opposed disorder and illegal violence, but believed he could win the forthcoming presidential elections. He had no inclination or reason to gamble on armed insurrection.

Nevertheless, Gaitán was in close contact with the Soviet Legation and with Communist leaders and, reportedly, accepted Russian money. A C.I.A. report from Colombia, written two and one-half months before the Bogotazo, stated:

JANUARY 29.—Mr. G.,[7] the leading Colombian Communist, who has been given the task of overthrowing the Pérez (Conservative) government, boasts that he can count on planes and artillery when necessary.[8] In Bogotá, this group has allegedly stored arms and explosives in 17 houses. Mr. G. is also reported the intermediary between the Soviet Legation and Gaitán, to whom he furnished money, supposedly for his Liberal movement.[9]

[5] It was in fact overthrown on November 24, 1948.
[6] Rafael Azula Barrera, *De la revolución al orden nuevo*, Editorial Kelly, Bogotá, 1956, pp. 334-5.
[7] Probably Antonio Garcia.
[8] This material was in fact made available from Venezuela by the Democratic Action group.
[9] Published in the press at the time and reprinted in Senate Internal Security Subcommittee, *op. cit.*, p. 116.

Gaitán had expected to be named a delegate to the Inter-American Conference, but he was not. The Communist
Party thought that resentment at this affront would induce
him to cooperate in their schemes to wreck the conference.
A Plenum of the Central Committee of the Party decided to
approach Gaitán openly with the proposal that he urge a
boycott of the conference. Gaitán, however, was not merely
a revolutionary visionary; he was also a man who hated
disorder and illegal action. He not only refused to have anything to do with the Communist plan, but publicly denounced the Reds and urged the public to take no part in
the projected boycott.[10]

This general picture is confirmed by Bernardo Ibañez,
Chilean President of the Inter-American Confederation of
Workers (the anti-Communist labor organization affiliated
with the AFL-CIO), who was present in Bogotá at the
time.

"Notwithstanding the fact that the Communists surrounded him with friendliness and flattery," Ibañez wrote,
"Gaitán maintained an independent and firm attitude with
them, as he stated publicly on the eve of the inauguration of
the IX Pan American Conference. In those days there was
talk in Bogotá that disturbances would occur and that the
stage was being set to sabotage the conference. Gaitán hastened to determine who was responsible and denounced the
planned provocations as acts against democracy and the
unity of the Americas. He stated his repudiation of such
acts." [11]

By March 24th, Gaitán had received a warning from
United States Ambassador Beaulac that the Communists
were planning to break up the conference and that, if they

---

[10] Alberto Niño H., *Antecedentes y secretos del 9 de abril*, Editorial Pax,
Bogotá, 1949, p. 23. This invaluable book is by the former Security Chief of
Colombia, a Liberal serving a Conservative government, and an exceptionally
intelligent director of security and counterespionage.

[11] Letter to Serafino Romualdi, published in part in *Inter-American Labor
News*, May 1948.

succeeded, the Liberal Party would probably be blamed." [12]

Now that Gaitán had clarified his position, he was regarded as an enemy by the organizers of the forthcoming insurrection. Venezuela now became the chief staging area both for the assembly of arms and the instruction of foreign subversive agents.

A great many Venezuelan arms were reaching Colombia. When some of these were seized by the forces under Security Chief Niño, the Venezuelan Government could no longer pretend ignorance. It officially advised the Colombian Government that arms had been stolen from its arsenals. It sent a list of the serial numbers of these "stolen" arms, covering machine guns, automatic pistols, rifles and revolvers. This explanation deceived nobody. Prominent leaders of the Colombian Liberal Party told Security Chief Niño that the Venezuelan Government had made firm promises of arms and fighting men to aid a Liberal revolution in Colombia. Furthermore, nobody was being very secretive about the matter.[13]

Despite Gaitán's belated, but firm, stand against violence, leftwing leaders of the Liberal Party were arming small groups of twenty people in the countryside and larger armed contingents in the cities. The plan was for the urban groups to contain the regular army while the rural combat units captured public buildings, barracks, telegraph offices, radio stations and arsenals. These small rural groups were also supposed to wipe out those who opposed the revolution and to arm the rural masses.

There was general theft of arms from public arsenals and from private stores. Liberal leaders managed to block the usual search methods and denied the Secret Service the right to shadow or interrogate suspects unless it first resorted to protracted and cumbersome judicial procedures.[14]

[12] U.S. News & World Report, April 23, 1948, pp. 13-14.
[13] Niño, op. cit., p. 23.
[14] Ibid, pp. 23ff.

The Colombian Communist leadership was unfit to lead an armed insurrection on the scale contemplated. It was split into two factions, both of which were poorly led. As Security Chief Niño put the matter: "International Communism doesn't take this stupid and ineffectual C.P. of ours seriously and, though the International Communists use and direct it without giving explanations, the international command despises the local Party and doesn't bother to hide the fact."

Consequently, preparations for the Bogotá uprising were placed in the hands of a key group of international Communist leaders and activists who were brought to Bogotá for the purpose, together with those Colombian Communists, for the most part undercover, who served as liaison elements between the Soviet Legation and the trade union elements. The Colombian unions were Communist-controlled and affiliated with the Red-dominated Confederation of Latin American Labor (CTAL).

According to Security Chief Niño, the foreigners who were involved in preparing the armed rising paid little attention to the local Communist Party leaders. They were in contact with Antonio Garcia and Gerardo Molina, who worked closely with the Russian Legation.

Fidel Castro in Bogotá

Security Chief Niño lists the following as foreign Communists implicated in the preparations for the Bogotá insurrection: Salvador Ocampo, Machado, Luis Fernandez Juan, Eugene Kerbaul, Milorad Pesic B., Frances MacKinnon Damon, Blas Roca, Rafael del Pino and Fidel Alejandro Castro.

In terms of the Red hierarchy, Castro was in distinguished company, for most of the nine alleged agents named by Niño were veteran Communists and either responsible Party leaders or seasoned Soviet agents.

Thus, Blas Roca was the General Secretary of the Cuban

Communist Party. Machado was probably Gustavo Machado, the leader of the Venezuelan Communist Party. Salvador Ocampo was one of the top Red leaders of Chile and also Secretary General of the Chilean Labor Federation. Luis Fernandez Juan has been characterized as a former "Red General" in the Spanish Civil War.[15] Milorad Pesic traveled on a French passport, but was a Yugoslavian agent of the Cominform.

As for Frances Damon, she was described as an American from a distinguished Honolulu family, who had lived in Moscow for years and was engaged in organizing the World Federation of Democratic Youth, a Communist-front organization. Both Fidel Castro and Rafael del Pino came to Bogotá with credentials from this organization.[16] Another Cuban Communist or fellow traveler, who came to Bogotá with Castro and worked with him, was Enrique Ovares Herrera.[17]

The trip of Castro and his fellow Cuban revolutionary, del Pino, had been financed by the movement of Argentine dictator Juan D. Perón, who, at the time, was cooperating closely with the Cominform. The two Cubans went to Caracas first, where they conferred with Rómulo Betancourt and received warm letters of recommendation from him. They arrived at the Medellín airport on March 29th[18] and were immediately placed under surveillance by the Colombian National Security Office. The reason for this surveillance, according to Niño, was:

"These two men came as replacements for two Russian agents stationed in Cuba, whose plans were known and who were expected by the Colombian police. Instead these two

---

[15] Venezuelan Catholic Youth and National Anti-Communist Front, *op. cit.*
[16] Niño, *op. cit.*, p. 50 and Fandiño Silva, *op cit.*, p. 33.
[17] Azula Barrera, *op. cit.*, p. 450.
[18] The ranks of this little band had already been thinned. Frances Damon and "General" Fernandez Juan had been observed at a secret meeting with a representative of the Russian Legation, whom the police had followed. They were warned not to engage in political activities. These two left Colombia, their usefulness presumably at an end, on March 27th.

came . . . Before the 9th of April, a telegram was taken
from them announcing the arrival of one of the Russians." [19]

Fidel Castro and the Murder of Gaitán

On September 22, 1949, *El Grafico* of Caracas published
an interesting and, for that matter sensational, report from
Colombian Detective #6 to the "Chief of the Intelligence
Services of the Armed Forces, General Staff of the Army"
entitled "General Antecedents of the Aliens of Cuban Nationality, Messrs. Fidel Castro and Rafael del Pino." This
police report was originally published in the influential Bogotá daily, *El Siglo*.[20] It deals with the results of the surveillance of Fidel Castro immediately prior to and during the
Bogotá uprising. The report not only links Castro with Communism, but connects him with the murder of Jorge Eliecer
Gaitán!

The authenticity of this report can scarcely be doubted.
It was published in the press of three Latin American countries and has never, to my knowledge, been challenged.
Moreover, it corresponds in essentials to other Colombian
intelligence material, available to the writer, which has been
authenticated. Nor can the report be explained away as a
police fabrication designed to smear Fidel Castro, since, in
1948 and 1949, Castro was not a person of sufficient political
stature to warrant such treatment.

Detective #6 stated that he was detailed by the Chief
of Detectives of the National Police, Dr. Ivan Arévalo, to
guard the President of the Republic, Dr. Mariano Ospina
Pérez, and his wife during an evening performance which
they were attending at the Colón Theatre on April 3rd.

At about 10 P.M., shortly after the third act of the play

---

[19] Niño, *op. cit.*, p. 77.
[20] It has been translated into English and published in *Carib*, Ciudad Trujillo,
Dominican Republic, No. 29 (June 1959), pp. 77-83. However, I have preferred to use my own translation.

had begun, "there was a shower of leaflets from the gallery. These had been printed in Havana; they lacked the Bogotá municipal tax stamp; they were definitely Communist in style and revolutionary phraseology and contrary to the democratic policies of our country, England and the United States."

With two other detectives, he proceeded to the gallery where he caught the two Cubans in the act of showering "the boxes and orchestra of the Colón Theatre with their revolutionary propaganda."

Detective #6 took Fidel Castro and del Pino into custody and proceeded to their lodgings—Room 33 of the Hotel Claridge. There the two Cubans voluntarily showed the detectives various papers, some of importance. There was a letter from Rómulo Betancourt "recommending both of them" and various Communist or leftwing books, including one by Betancourt "with whom they claimed to have close relationships of friendship and political affinity."

Castro and del Pino claimed that their object was to unify the Latin American students and to bring pressure on the Ninth Inter-American Conference for the freedom of all European colonial possessions in Ibero-America. (This was an issue being raised vigorously by Argentine dictator Juan Perón with international Communist support.)

The detectives wanted written authorization to pick up the passports of the Cubans and summon them before the Bureau of Detectives of the National Police where they could be interrogated concerning their alleged Communist activities. This permission was denied.

However, Castro and del Pino were informed that their passports had been visaed for the Medellín airport only and not for Bogotá. They were directed to report to Dr. Camilo Cortés Zapata, the Chief of the Alien Section of the National Police, on Monday.

When Monday passed without either of them showing up, Dr. Cortés decided to go personally to their room in the

Hotel Claridge in the company of Detective #6. Castro and del Pino were there.

Detective #6 reported: ". . . I was particularly interested to see on the table which served as a desk for the two Cubans a photograph of Dr. Jorge Eliecer Gaitán, together with various leaflets with photographs of him and other publications apparently written by him, also with his picture. When I asked del Pino why he had this picture and this printed matter, he replied that students who were followers of Gaitán had given them to him, and that, for the rest, they did not know Gaitán, were not in agreement with his political views and had no interest in them."

The police would soon discover that this explanation was a lie. They would then begin to wonder whether Castro and del Pino had acquired these photographs so that they could memorize Gaitán's physical appearance in connection with his forthcoming assassination.

There was also a cable in code which the detectives were unable to decipher. It read: "La Habana, Cuba, 3 de abril de 1948—FAL-PINO. Bogotá. Hotel Claridge. Seguro. Esa Diez. En punto. IGLESIAS." [21] The next morning, the two Cubans appeared at the office of the Chief of the Alien Section. "When they were interrogated about the cablegram, they became extremely rattled, but were unable to give a sensible answer." They were informed by Dr. Cortés that it was illegal for aliens to intervene in any way in the internal affairs of Colombia. After they had promised not to do so, the detectives let them go.

This was the 6th of April. As Detective #6 left the two Cubans on the street, "a friend of mine named Bermudez greeted me and asked me who the two boys were and said that he had seen them the day before in the offices of Dr. Jorge Eliecer Gaitán."

The Cubans had lied about not knowing Gaitán. They also

[21] FAL-PINO. Bogotá. Hotel Claridge. Certain. That ten. On the dot. IGLESIAS.

lied about their movements. As they were leaving Detective #6, del Pino said that they were headed for the Hotel Granada, but Castro "obviously agitated" told del Pino he was mistaken. At 11 that morning, Detective #6 "ran into them in the place they were not going to—the lobby of the Granada."

The report continues: "This was the state of affairs until the tragic day, the 9th of the present month. Again in the morning, hurrying to make some arrests, I was on Highway 7 near the Granada. There, in the Colombia Cafe, seated at a table with two other people were the Cubans. It was 11:30 A.M. I am sure that I am not mistaken. There is another witness to the scene, Detective Diego Quiñones Olarte, who heard the Cubans talk about the way I had arrested them and heard them mention my name. *Moments later, with Detective Quiñones Olarte, I saw del Pino standing in the door of the Colombia Cafe, talking with a shabbily dressed individual whose photograph would later appear in the newspapers as the murderer of Dr. Gaitán.*" [22]

This conference between the assassin of Gaitán, Roa Sierra, and the Cuban student, del Pino, reportedly occurred about an hour and a half before the murder. It is safe to assume that the murderer did not spend the two hours before his crime in casual conversations with strangers. Nor is it easy to conjecture an innocent reason for a meeting between the pro-Communist intellectual, del Pino, and the pro-fascist drifter, Roa Sierra.

After Fidel Castro took power in Cuba, the lawyer for former Colombian dictator, Rojas Pinilla, Daniel Valois Arcé stated, according to an A.P. dispatch of February 19, 1959, that "Fidel Castro and another Cuban by the name of Rafael del Pino had been seen by a detective a few days prior to the murder in the company of Roa Sierra."

Contemporary press dispatches add weight to this charge. On April 19, 1948, ten days after the blood bath, the United

<hr>

[22] My emphasis—N.W.

Press quoted *El Tiempo* of Bogotá that "Roa was seen in the company of several people who appeared to be foreigners, a few days prior to the crime."

According to Fandiño Silva: "Castro's correspondence was secretly sent to the house of Olimpia Castro—No. 5-48A, South 11th Street, Bogotá. Among his papers was found a plan of the Capitol, the conference site, with pencilled markings showing the locations of the Dominican and Chilean delegations. The rioters of April 9th were able to get as far as there." [23] The reason for singling out these two Legations, presumably for destruction by the enraged, blood-lustful mob, was political. The Dominican Republic, under the dictatorial regime of General Trujillo, was a special object of Communist hatred. The Chilean situation was somewhat different. Six months before these events, Chilean President Gabriel Gonzáles Videla had dismissed the Communist members of his cabinet, broken diplomatic relations with the Soviet Union, Czechoslovakia and Yugoslavia, smashed Communist-led strikes, arrested 200 of the country's top Communist leaders and branded the Party as totally "at the service of the political, economic and military interests" of the Soviet Union.

Security Chief Alberto Niño found several things about the two Cuban "students" interesting. Surveillance disclosed that they had no contact with the open leaders of the puny and despised Colombian Communist Party, but that they did meet secretly with Antonio García and other undercover Colombian Communists who served as liaison between the Soviet Legation and the trade union Communist militants. A letter to Fidel Castro from "Mirtha" was seized by the police.[24] It was chiefly amatory, but contained the sentence: "I remember that you told me you were going to start a revo-

[23] Fandiño Silva, *op. cit.*, pp. 43ff.
[24] Mirtha Diaz Balart was Fidel Castro's fiancée whom he would marry later that year.

lution in Bogotá." The letter was seized on April 3rd, the armed rising erupted on April 9th.

Security Chief Niño also considered it highly pertinent that the two Cubans had stopped off at Venezuela first, receiving recommendations and financial aid from Betancourt, because, "Nearly all incoming foreign Communists went first to Venezuela."

On April 8th, Castro and del Pino held a meeting with militants of the Colombian Labor Federation (CTC) on the techniques of the general strike and armed seizure of power (golpe de estado). "Those who attended took notes. Castro and del Pino agreed to give another lecture the next day. However, their arrest was ordered and they did not return." [25]

From Murder to Insurrection

On the next day, the 9th, the assassination occurred and the planned uprising of the masses instantly followed. Jorge Eliecer Gaitán was shot to death in the business district of the city at lunchtime on April 9, 1948. The actual murder was described as follows by Guillermo Pérez Sarmiento, Director of the United Press in Colombia, who was an eyewitness:

". . . I was in the Tivoli Bar, at the corner of San Francisco, with Alberto Merino-Arquila and Armando Moyse, when we heard with complete clarity the shots, three one right after the other and the last after an interval. A few moments later, the popular Nepumeceno Barajas entered screaming, his face completely changed: 'They have just assassinated Dr. Gaitán.'

"Forgetting my hat, I went out hurriedly, followed by Merino. I saw a large group near the door of the Agustin Nieto Building to which all sorts of people were running

[25] Niño, *op. cit.*, p. 77.

from all directions. Opening for myself a passageway and pushing several people aside, I was able to find Jorge Eliecer Gaitán stretched on the ground: the head twisted on the shoulder, the face covered with the pallor of death, the open hand stretched out toward the sidewalk. I bent over in consternation and cried out, 'My God, what has happened, Jorge?,' touching his face, but he did not open his eyes. Now that I was closer, I could see that he was lying in an enormous pool of blood. I pushed back the hair on his forehead and helped to lift him; just then a black taxi, breaking all traffic rules, arrived, having crossed Jiménez Avenue going south. When we lifted him, probably because of a wave of blood to the brain, he opened his eyes and contracted his mouth in a grimace which seemed to me to be a smile. Then he closed them again. I will never be able to forget this glance filled with sorrow and sweetness . . . It was one-twenty in the afternoon; five minutes had passed since the attack.

"I was standing on a greasy hat. I leaned over and picked it up. Somebody came up to me, saying, 'It is the assassin's!' He asked me to give it to him. People standing in front of the pool of blood began to cry like children, sobbing. I recognized the professor of penology, Mariano Lopez Lucas, whose face was bathed in tears. Sorrow overcame me and I felt a lump in my throat, but I controlled it and went to the door of the Granada Drugstore. The assassin was there between two policemen; he had turned his greenish face away and seemed to be gripped by panic in the face of the growing popular indignation around him. Anger mounted, though its first expressions were only those of hatred and mistrust. He was poorly dressed and my attention was caught by the blue tie with red stripes and the enormous amount of hair which he had. I saw Eduardo Lozano, the lottery ticket seller, hit him and grab him by the hair. Other people hit him. I tried to thrust myself between him and the crowd, calling out, 'Don't kill him; he is more useful alive.' Others tried to do the same. But soon the indignation grew greater and the insignificant little man—who gave me the impression of being an impassioned fanatic—fell to the ground, and they all fought for a turn to kick him. Soon he was torn to pieces.

"At my side, a 15-year-old boy cleaned the tip of his shoe with a piece of paper after having kicked the assassin. A voice cried, 'To the Palace!' and the macabre dragging of the dying man began. At that moment, I understood clearly the fury of the populace which justifies everything and the irreparable error (the killing of the murderer) which had taken place before me and which history would condemn, though perhaps it would also justify it. . . .

"Then I ran precipitately to All American Cables where I sent the first dispatches telling the outside world of the death of Jorge Eliecer Gaitán." [26]

Another eyewitness, Plinio Mendoza Neira, was interviewed by Azula Barrera about the assassination and said:
". . . it was so dramatic, brutal and surprising that I can barely reconstruct it. I had to speak to Gaitán about something urgent. I went to his office at noon, but met him leaving with friends . . . I invited him then, in the presence of all of them, to lunch in a restaurant." Gaitán accepted and they left the office. "When we reached the main door (of the office building, I took Gaitán's arm and as we moved a little away from our friends, I said,

" 'What I have to say to you is very brief.'

"I suddenly felt that Gaitán was pulling back, trying to cover his face with his hands and trying to get back to the office building. Simultaneously, I heard three consecutive shots and then another one fractions of a second later. Gaitán fell to the ground. I bent over to help him without being able to avoid the immense surprise that this absurd occurrence caused me.

" 'What happened, Jorge?' I asked.

[26] Quoted in Francisco Fandiño Silva, op. cit., pp. 15ff.

"He didn't answer. He was transformed, the eyes half-opened, a bitter grimace on his lips and his hair in disorder, while a thread of blood ran under his head.

"Pedro Eliseo Cruz examined him. The situation was very serious. We picked him up quickly and, taking the first taxi that we saw, we took him to the central clinic."

Plinio Mendoza was asked by Azula Barrera about the assassin:

"I cannot say exactly. Everything had the speed of lightning. I know that he tried to take refuge in the adjacent drugstore, but the people, infuriated, grabbed him and put an end to him, kicking him and then dragging him through the streets to the Palace. They say that by the time they left him, he was a human rag, a piece of shapeless flesh, unrecognizable." [27]

There were three bullet holes in the body of Gaitán, all of them mortal—in the base of the neck, the lungs and the liver. Yet Gaitán lived for an hour after the attack, since he was an unusually strong man, a man who exercised daily, kept a strict regimen, was very narcissistic and under the constant care of a doctor. After the attack, all of the leaders of the Liberal Party stayed with him at the clinic until he died. At this time, the burning and looting was already going on.[28]

Azula Barrera probably investigated the crime more carefully than any other official. He has this to say about it:

"Juan Roa Sierra was small, insignificant, pale-faced, his face angular and weak; he had been unshaven for several days and he was dressed miserably with a gray trenchcoat and a blue tie with red stripes—all this according to the eyewitnesses who saw him moments after the crime was committed, while he was trying to hide behind the bars of the

[27] Rafael Azula Barrera, *De la revolución al orden nuevo*, Editorial Kelly, Bogotá, 1956, pp. 374-5.
[28] *Ibid*, p. 379.

Granada Drugstore, still holding a long revolver which was .38 caliber and still smoking . . . The details of the crime, the circumstances of the death, the diversity of the accounts given by witnesses concerning the identity of the killer, all aroused the most extraordinary doubts.

"From the first moment, there was question as to whether the man taken by the crowd was really the killer or not. As Roa Sierra ran, two policemen followed, and Carlos A. Jiménez took his revolver away. When questioned, he said only two things: 'Don't talk to me; don't you see that I am incommunicado?' and, when asked why he had fired the shot, 'the highest motives.'

"The effort to save him was useless. The crowd grew in size and menace, so that the drugstore was forced to open its iron shutters. A lottery ticket vendor was the first to punch him and grab him by the hair. Then the bootblacks moved in with their small boxes and beat his face to pieces. The sight of blood roused the crowd even more and they ripped off his pathetic clothing, carrying the pieces as torn and bloody banners as they dragged the dying man through the streets. A voice was heard then, 'To the Palace! Let the bosses see the barbarian assassins hired by the Government!'

"And then the macabre parade began, feverishly, through the Calle Real, dragging that almost shapeless corpse, of which the ghastly face showed only one half-opened eye, since the other, destroyed by a blow, had been converted into a clot of blood. A menacing, heterogeneous mass, uttering cries of hate, followed the procession, and, between curses and broken phrases, some approached to kick the dead man, some to spit on him, others to soil him with obscene words, but most to wound him further with knives. Like a man-beast, the crowd crushed with terrible anger the hand which had wielded the weapon that brought on the tragedy. . . . This was the implacable force of anarchy, the law of turmoil and the street, anonymous, irresponsible, continuous, which brings to the surface all the filth of the lower depths." [29]

To quote Taine:

"The group whose purpose is violent action is composed not only of the most miserable, of the most exalted, of those most inclined toward destruction and license, but also, since it is carrying out a violent action, of the most brutal, the most unreasoning and the most perverse of mankind. It descends even further, into utter darkness and into the most abject forms of ferocity and madness. In effect, for a man who has given and received blows to be able to resist the intoxication of murder and not use his strength as a savage does, he must be used to arms and danger, the habit of shedding blood coldly, the sentiment of honor, above all the memory of that terrible military code, which in the imagination of each soldier keeps the gallows in sight and makes his ascent to it certain should he step out of line.

"All these interior and exterior brakes are lacking in the man launched in mutiny. He is a novice in the road he follows. He does not fear the law, since he is above it. The act which he has started drags him further than he wishes. His anger is increased by danger and resistance. Fever attacks him as he goes with the feverish; he follows the bandits who have become his comrades. Add to this the noises, the drunkenness, the sight of destruction, the physical vibration of the nervous system in a tension greater than it can bear, and you will understand how the peasant, the worker, the bourgeois, overcome by civilization, revert to barbarism, become worse than a primitive animal, worse than the primitive ape who kills as he capers, lewd, gesturing and bloody . . ." [30]

A few minutes after the murder of Gaitán, a leaflet was

[29] *Ibid*, pp. 390-1.
[30] Quoted by Azula Barrera, *op. cit.*, pp. 390-1; hence my English version is translated from the Spanish rather than directly from the French.

distributed in the streets of Bogotá. No less than six different type faces had been used in its preparation; the paper on which it was printed was dry; the margins were neat, and there were no ink smudges. It read:

"The assassin's government of Ospina Pérez, which ordered one of its wicked butchers to put an end to the life of the great leader of Colombian democracy (Gaitán), is now trying to make the people swallow the most vile and odious calumny, accusing the Communists of this monstrous attempt. They lie, a thousand times, these assassins! Liberals and Communists, united in this historic hour of our country, will save democracy by overthrowing this assassins' government and creating a revolutionary junta which will assume power. In the popular militia of the armed people, Liberals, Communists and democrats in general, united as a whole, will form a people's army which will re-establish democracy in Colombia. Down with the barbarian murderers and liars! All democratic forces united against reaction!" [31]

[31] Quoted by Azula Barrera, *op. cit.*, pp. 390-1.

2

The Saturnalia of Blood

"In this fight against natural chaos, the guilt of society is that it is a society. The guilt is order, and the guilty are those whose authority imposes order. If the scapegoat is to shoulder this sin, then it is a farce to have him a child or a broken-down prostitute. Only the man of authority can expiate the sin of order."

—J. Bronowski
The Face of Violence[1]

THE mob had disposed of the putative assassin, mercilessly and instantly. It had moved on him with terrifying speed and cruelty, beating and stomping his face into an unrecognizable, livid mass, stripping him of all his clothes except for the necktie and dragging his naked and faceless body toward the Presidential Palace, which was already besieged by crowds "who apparently were intent upon entering and assassinating the President."[2]

[1] George Braziller, New York, 1955, p. 15.
[2] Willard L. Beaulac, *Career Ambassador*, Macmillan, New York, 1951, p. 243.

Juan Roa Sierra was a 25-year-old unskilled loiterer and drifter, a man who was very poor and who came from a very poor family. He sometimes got odd jobs and kept alive by sleeping with a much older woman. His opinions were violently right-wing, but he was a person with no known political affiliations. If Roa Sierra murdered Gaitán on his own account, the political motive was not that the Liberal Party leader had finally broken with the Communists, but that he had remained a left-winger and the idol of the Bogotá proletariat.

But did Roa Sierra act on his own account? Did he in fact commit the murder at all?

Reconstructing the crime 15 days later, Milton Bracker of the *New York Times* asked himself whether Roa Sierra had accomplices who stood by ostensibly to protect him, but actually to silence and kill him. Ambassador Beaulac had similar doubts.

"Did Roa Sierra act on his own," he wrote in his memoirs, "or was he the simple-minded tool of others? Was his act an ordinary crime, or did it have a political motive? These questions cannot yet be answered.

"Roa Sierra was beaten to death by witnesses of his crime minutes after he had committed it. Was Roa killed by persons so outraged by the crime he had committed that they could not help exacting retribution then and there? Or was his death instigated or caused by persons anxious that he not live to testify concerning the reasons for his act? It is not possible to answer these questions either, and it may never be possible to answer them." [3]

The area of doubt is even broader. According to Rafael Azula Barrera, who was at the time General Secretary of the Colombian Presidency, President Ospina Pérez and his top advisers analyzed the murder and reached the conclusion that Roa Sierra had definitely been killed in order to be kept silent. The revolver which Roa Sierra was carrying was later

[3] Beaulac, *op. cit.*, p. 253.

demonstrated to be incapable of firing the accurate shots which killed Gaitán.[4] Furthermore, Roa Sierra was not trained in the use of small arms. It is also interesting that the eyewitnesses quoted in the previous chapters heard the shots and saw Gaitán fall to the ground, but they did not see Roa Sierra fire them. If Azula Barrera's extraordinary conclusions are correct, a possible implication is that Roa Sierra was paid, or in some other way persuaded, to stand in the street with a revolver which had recently been fired in order to give the real assassin time to escape. Since Roa Sierra had once been in a mental institution,[5] it is quite possible that he could have been cajoled into this dangerous and foolhardy action.

If Roa Sierra was killed by Communist agents, it is obviously important to know who was in the immediate vicinity at the time of the crime. According to Azula Barrera, a Colombian detective's report stated that Fidel Castro, Rafael del Pino and Enrique Ovares Herrera were seen in the vicinity of the Agustín Nieto Building, speaking in low voices with a group of well-known Communist agitators.[6] The third Cuban, Enrique Ovares, was recognized as the man wearing a tan coat with white stripes who fled precipitately a few minutes after the assassination of Gaitán in a taxi that was fortuitously close.[7]

These items of circumstantial evidence are not sufficient to convict Castro and his associates of complicity in the murder of Gaitán and the destruction of his reputed killer, but they are sufficient to create well-grounded suspicion. It is also of interest that neither del Pino nor Ovares are in a position to shed further light on these matters, since both men are at present (August 1960) political prisoners of Fidel Castro.

[4] Azula Barrera, *op. cit.*, pp. 390-1.
[5] Beaulac writes: "a miserable drifter of a person who had once been an inmate of an insane asylum." *op. cit.*, p. 253.
[6] Azula Barrera, *op. cit.*, p. 450.
[7] *Ibid*, pp. 390-1.

Finally, the fact that Roa Sierra was killed primarily by the bootblacks who smashed his face in with their wooden boxes means nothing, since it would have been easy for the Communists to equip a few activists with these boxes.

According to Azula Barrera, President Ospina Pérez and his Cabinet assigned responsibility for the armed rising to the Communists and Betancourt's Democratic Action for the following reasons: (1) The leaflet, absolving the Communist Party of blame for Gaitán's murder, appeared on the streets in thousands of copies within minutes of the assassination. (2) A large number of foreign leftists, from Mexico, Guatemala, Cuba, the Dominican Republic, Venezuela, Yugoslavia and Russia, many on diplomatic passports, had assembled in Bogotá shortly before the operation. (3) The Soviet Legation had built up a staff of 200 persons, far in excess of its legitimate functions. (4) The presence of the Cuban "students"— Castro, del Pino and Ovares and the suspicious conduct of the last at the time of the murder. (5) The fact that Roa Sierra was instantly killed. (6) The crossing of the Colombian northern border at the time of the troubles by 500 stalwarts of Betancourt's Democratic Action, armed with aircraft, armored cars, machine guns and Red Cross trucks.[8]

There are other reasons to believe that the assassination of Gaitán was planned and executed by the international Communist apparatus. Elaborate preparations had been made on a technical level for the armed uprising. What was needed was an overwhelming grievance which would arouse the masses and send them out in the streets to fight. Moreover, if the insurrection was to have a good chance of success, it could not have been delayed.

The reason for this was that the Colombian Army, comprising 10,000 soldiers, could be counted on to uphold the constitutional government, as in fact it did. The operation, therefore, had to be timed for the brief period in which 80%

[8] *Ibid*, pp 390-1.

of the Army was mustered out and replaced by raw, untrained, inexperienced recruits. Concerning this matter, Ambassador Beaulac wrote:

"Gaitán's death had been diabolically timed to coincide with the lowest point in strength and efficiency that the Colombian Army had reached in many years. Furthermore, of the 2,000 soldiers that should have been in the Bogotá area that day, 1,400 were outside the area engaged in military exercises. Colombian Army leaders could not help believing that these coincidences had been planned." [9]

Finally, the overriding Soviet propaganda purpose was to force the suspension of the Inter-American Conference. This obviously required that the blow be struck before the Conference adjourned.

From the Communist standpoint, Dr. Gaitán was the only completely logical victim. He was the idol of the Colombian masses and his murder would be sure to stir them as the death of no other person could. Writing of the shabby, impoverished people who raged into the streets after the murder, Beaulac observed: "They were Gaitán's people, those to whom he had addressed his special appeal. They were the 'proletariat' of Russia, the 'shirtless ones' of Argentina, the 'masses' of Colombia, who, Gaitán had said, would inherit the earth." [10]

In addition, Gaitán was, from the Communist standpoint, a renegade and a traitor. He had been in the confidence of the Party; he had received money for his movement from the Soviet Legation. When asked to cooperate with the Soviet program, he had not only refused, but had denounced the Red plan to wreck the Conference to the public and to the police. This made him a turncoat, a man deserving of death.

[9] Beaulac, *op. cit.*, p. 250.
[10] *Ibid.*, pp. 241-2.

The Organized Holocaust

The revolution moved forward with the ghastly precision of a wave of molten lava. Its individual elements were seething, hungry people, driven by frustration, rage, blood-lust, sadism, greed and drunkenness. Yet it was directed, according to a plan that had been carefully worked out in every major detail, by leaders who remained apart from the emotional orgies of the mob.

"The destruction of the civic center of the city was complete," wrote Azula Barrera. "As though laid waste by implacable bombing, it had been reduced to ruins, even concrete buildings which ordinarily require whole weeks to be wrecked by the normal techniques of demolition. European cities, precision bombed during the last War, might perhaps have offered a similar spectacle. Neither Guernica nor Irun, nor Toledo, nor even the University City of Madrid (punished so ruthlessly by Franco) presented such a Dante-esque vision of desolation and ruin as Bogotá after a few hours of the fury of the multitude.

"It would not have been easy to throw to the ground in a few minutes whole buildings of reinforced concrete unless large quantities of gasoline and tools of tremendous destructive power had been used. The strongest and most secure locks of houses and warehouses were torn to pieces in minutes by a secret process of terrible efficiency. Dauntless individuals, leading isolated groups, took it upon themselves to open everything instantly in this way, even to the most carefully sealed off buildings. Then they left them to the action of the crowd. When the sacking was completed, they threw incendiary bombs into the devastated places, which produced a long flame of a pale blue color. The walls, sprayed with gasoline, burned in a matter of seconds. In this way, they attacked first the hardware stores,[11] then the

11 To get knives, machetes and other weapons.

liquor stores, then the large luxury shops, furriers, jewelers, silversmiths, all establishments which displayed articles of high value brilliantly—the most precious stones, the most coveted works of art, attractive, stylish novelties—in short, everything that flatters vanity and embellishes modern life." [12]

Thus, there seem to have been four waves of destroyers: first, the special squads that tore open the locks and smashed open the doors with some special instrument which Azula Barrera was not able to describe; second, the disorganized mob of looters and vandals; third, the squads which sprayed the walls of the gutted buildings with gasoline, and, finally, the actual arsonists who threw incendiaries into the inflammable, gasoline-drenched edifices.

The cold-blooded, methodical manner in which this destruction by fire was organized and executed was one of several factors which convinced Ambassador Beaulac that the entire Bogotazo was a carefully planned Communist operation. He wrote:

"There was one phenomenon reported by numerous observers on April 9, and that was that the burnings that took place were organized. They were carried out by small groups of men. The groups carried gasoline and equipment for spreading it around. Some carried sprayers such as those used for spraying trees. Each group had a leader, and each leader had a list of buildings that the group was to set on fire. Some of the lists were typewritten. These groups went into action immediately after Gaitán's death. This leads to the presumption that the burnings were planned before Gaitán was killed. Is there anything in the history of the Liberal Party to suggest that Liberals deliberately planned the burnings? Is there anything in the history of the Conservative Party to suggest that the Conservatives planned them? There is nothing. Is there anything in the history of

[12] Azula Barrera, *op. cit.*, pp. 376-7.

International Communism to suggest that the Communists might have done it? There is plenty." [13]

As in other Communist-directed operations of this character, the criminal classes were released from the prisons to give impetus to the work of destruction and forces were deployed at once against the places where police dossiers and political archives were stored so that these could be destroyed.

"From the first moment, all the prisons of the capital had been opened by the mutineers. Thus, the initial mass, assembled for the undeniable purpose of taking power, was made up of the lower social classes supplemented by the thousands of escaped prisoners . . . For this reason, the prime object of their destructiveness was the Palace of Justice, which was demolished to its very foundations, where all the most important records of both civil and criminal proceedings were kept. Later they burned the office of investigation of the National Police, disposing by fire of all files, office machinery and means of identifying aliens. Then their fury was turned on Catholic monuments. The Cathedral, the Archbishop's Palace, the Palace of the Papal Nuncio, the ancient temple of the Hospicio, all of the colleges of the Jesuits were soon food for the flames . . . To this was added the impressive sight of the looters fleeing to the hills, carrying heavy merchandise on their shoulders. Women . . . with bare feet . . . wearing stylish and expensive furs over their rags and exhibiting on their blackened hands the most luxurious of jewels . . . men who carried on their backs the almost inconceivable burden of refrigerators . . . and large machines . . . ragged children, selling for a few pennies bottles of the finest liquors, exquisite silver, costly clothing. A long tragic parade and an open market in the destroyed streets with their accumlated ruins and corpses, the faces of which were lighted by the crackling flames of

[13] Beaulac, *op. cit.*, pp. 255-6.

fires which successive torrents of rain had been unable to extinguish." [14]

Another important witness was Bernardo Ibañez, the Chilean labor leader. He wrote:

"Fifteen minutes after the attack on Gaitán, all the radio broadcasting stations in Bogotá were taken over by the Communists through workers and students. The radio stations were inciting the people to revolt against the Government, against the conference, against Yankee imperialism, etc. Precise instructions were being issued to plunder arms deposits, hardware stores and gunsmiths' shops, the department stores, the Government buildings, the police precincts and the army barracks. An hour later the crowd, instigated by the Communists, invaded the capitol or Parliament Building, where the Pan-American Conference was being held, destroying the luxurious equipment with which it had been furnished. But the incident that attracted my attention most was the fact that the rioters concentrated on the destruction of the offices of the Chilean and U.S. delegations. In my opinion, this was due to the firm anticommunistic attitude of these two delegations. The Chilean and U.S. flags were trampled upon by the crowd, while the documents, typewriters, file cabinets, etc., were being destroyed or plundered . . .

"The orders that were given to the people, the propaganda carried over the radio broadcasts, the method of plundering to be put into practice, the unusual activity shown by the Soviet Legation during the first moments of the events, etc., all prove that this assassination was a coldblooded and ferocious international act of incitement conducted by the Russians on the weak democracy of Colombia, against the interests of the people of the Americas."[15]

Within hours of Gaitán's assassination, *El Popular,* the newspaper of Betancourt's political party in Venezuela, Dem-

[14] Azula Barrera, *op. cit.,* p. 378.
[15] Ibañez, *op. cit.*

ocratic Action, came out with a special edition hailing the Colombian revolution.

"Through the streets of the city," it proclaimed, "marched liberal students and among them was our great national leader *RÓMULO BETANCOURT*, Chief of the Venezuelan Delegation to the Ninth Inter-American Conference . . . It is understood that, as a consequence of the murder of Gaitán, *there has been launched the most bloody civil war ever seen in Colombia. The people have hurled themselves into the streets with appropriate violence and are seeking vengeance.*" [16]

Daily Worker special correspondent Joseph Starobin also praised the uprising which had brought destruction and agony upon the Colombian people. What gave Starobin and his readers additional pleasure was his belief that these events had damaged the prestige and power of the democracy of which he was at least nominally a citizen. He exulted that "Interruption of the Foreign Ministers' parley is a sock in the jaw to the big business men of the State Department . . . the world has suddenly seen America's feet of clay." [17]

The Role of Fidel Castro

Castro joined the insurrectionaries immediately, according to his adulatory biographer, Jules Dubois, and obtained a rifle from the Colombian police, most of whom were disloyal to their government.[18] He allegedly proceeded to the Eleventh Precinct, the headquarters of the rebel police elements and harangued them in favor of militant action. Dubois adds that he was ignored.

The Liberals demanded that Conservative President Ospina Pérez resign, but the latter refused. Throughout the

[16] My emphasis—N.W.
[17] *Daily Worker*, April 12, 1948, p. 3.
[18] Jules Dubois, *Fidel Castro*, Bobbs-Merrill, Indianapolis, 1959, p. 20. The version given here is almost certainly Fidel Castro's own story of the events.

ordeal, he showed moral and physical courage of an extraordinary sort. His political solution was to reorganize his Cabinet on a coalition basis immediately, giving the War Department to a Conservative, Justice to a Liberal and dividing the other Ministries equally. Ospina Pérez retained the Presidency in his own hands.

About 136 buildings worth $21,150,000 had already been destroyed in Bogotá. Historic churches had been gutted. For days no public mass could be celebrated in a devoutly Catholic city. In Barranquilla, the Red hammer and sickle was flying over the town hall.

The Liberal Party agreed to share power because its responsible leaders were appalled at the havoc and destruction which the Communist-led mob had been able to wreak in a bare 24 hours. It was essential to restore order, to get public utilities running again, to break the political strikes, to bury over a thousand corpses, to start cleaning up the rubble and devastation, to see that the Inter-American Conference was able to resume its sessions without running the risk of having its delegates murdered—in short, to return to civilization and order.

However, the Communists and other extremists continued the armed struggle. They did so because they had no interest in bringing peace to their country or bringing the Liberal Party into the Cabinet. They wanted havoc and continuing civil war. They hoped that they might be able to move through that havoc toward a revolutionary dictatorship.

According to Dubois, Castro fought in the hills by the side of these elements for 24 hours, until his ammunition was exhausted. When he returned, he discovered that President Ospina Pérez, in a nationwide broadcast, "had denounced the Cuban students in Bogotá as 'Communists' and had accused them of playing a leading role in the frustrated uprising." [19]

[19] *Ibid*, p. 22.

However, there is grave doubt that Fidel Castro ever went into the hills. The Dubois story may merely be one of the many instances in which Castro fabricated and distorted facts in order to place himself in a more or less heroic posture.

The valuable report of Detective #6 sheds a very different light on Castro's comportment during the Bogotázo. On the evening of April 13th, four days after the outbreak of the riots, Detective #6 was ordered to proceed to the Hotel Claridge with two associates and arrest the Cubans. He learned from the hotel manager, however, that they had paid their bills and left for the Cuban Legation that morning. The hotel manager also told Detective #6:

"That on the night of the 9th, they had arrived armed with rifles or shotguns and revolvers and with a good haul of loot which they were hardly able to cram into their valises." [20] The manager added that Castro talked on the phone in English that night with various people and "that in the last two days of his (Castro's) stay in that hotel, he was so preoccupied and nervous that he even begged the hotel manager to hide them in a secret place."

The detectives found a "carnet, which the office of Detectives now has in its possession, with a photograph of the two Cubans, identifying them as first-grade agents of the Third Front of the U.S.S.R. in South America." [21] At that time, the expression "third front" in the vocabulary of international Communism referred to activities designed to sway governments and peoples from the Free World alliance to neutralism. In other words, it concerned action directed specifically against the foreign policy of the United States. The disruption of an Inter-American conference fell into this category.

There is another intriguing bit of evidence—a United

[20] In his account, Dubois has Castro "appalled" at the looting of Bogotá stores and intervening without success "to persuade them (the looters) to stop . . . ," op. cit., p. 20.
[21] My emphasis—N.W.

Press dispatch by a Colombian correspondent who was an eyewitness to the police search. This read:

TWO CUBANS DISTRIBUTE ARMS
by Lacides Orozco

BOGOTÁ, Colombia, April 19 (1948) (United)—This morning, when I was sitting in the lounge of the Claridge Hotel, where I stay when in Bogotá, two detectives came in asking where they could find the manager. When they were received in the office, they said they were looking for two Cubans, Fidel Castro and Rafael del Pino, who had been staying at the hotel.

The two detectives took possession of the Cubans' correspondence, *which they opened in my presence,* and said that they were in possession of reliable information to the effect that Castro and del Pino had been leading the looting on the 9th April on the occasion of the assassination of the Liberal leader, Jorge Eliecer Gaitán.

The correspondence showed that both Cubans belonged to the Cuban Communist Party, and the letters, which are dated Havana 9th April, mention the Bogotá riots.[22]

The police report identifies the Cubans as Soviet agents; the Orozco account labels them members of the Cuban Communist Party. In an effort to find out from Orozco exactly what he recalled about these documents, I wrote him in care of the United Press, Bogotá, in May 1960.

On May 18th, Mr. Carlos J. Villar-Borda, the director of the United Press in Bogotá, was kind enough to reply at length. He informed me that Orozco was no longer with the organization. He added that Orozco had been brought in from Cartagena to help cover the Inter-American Conference, that he stayed at the same hotel as Castro and del Pino, that he became good friends of theirs, introduced them at the United Press and that, on the night of the Bogotázo, Castro and del Pino arrived at the U. P. Bureau armed.

[22] My emphasis—N.W.

Castro and del Pino found safe haven in the Cuban Legation just in time to avoid being arrested by the Colombian authorities as Communist agents and instigators of the armed rising. Dr. Guillermo Belt, the head of Cuba's delegation to the Inter-American Conference, arranged to have them flown back to Cuba.

In the Cuban Legation, del Pino boasted of having killed a priest during the fighting. Back in Havana, Castro bragged to the students about his part in the rioting and claimed he had personally killed two or three priests, whom he referred to as "black scavengers." Actually, no priests were killed in the Bogotázo and the Castro boast was significant merely as indicating his virulent hatred of the clergy.

The State Department and the Bogotázo

Bogotá provided massive circumstantial evidence of Fidel Castro's early affiliation with International Communism. Security Chief Niño referred to "the known Communists, Fidel Castro and Rafael del Pino." The President of Colombia, Mariano Ospina Pérez, denounced the Cubans as "Communists" and organizers of the insurrection in a nationwide radio speech delivered a few days after the tragedy. The distinguished Colombian reporter, Fandiño Silva, also named Castro as one of the International Communist agents who prepared and helped direct the rising.[23] The Colombian National Police reports showed that Fidel Castro had arrived in Bogotá to replace a known Russian agent; that he distributed Communist leaflets; that he communicated in code and used a mail drop; that he gave a lecture to Communist activists on the techniques of the coup d'etat; that he had advance knowledge of the planned uprising; that he knew Gaitán, but lied to the police about it; that he and his friends had numerous photographs of Gaitán in their possession, although they claimed to have no interest in

[23] op. cit., p. 33.

either the man or his ideas; that Castro's associate, del Pino, was in conference with Gaitán's killer less than two hours before the assassination took place; that Castro was near the scene of the crime in the company of well-known Communists; that Castro's associate, Ovares, fled a few minutes after the crime under suspicious circumstances; that documents were found in Fidel Castro's room identifying him and del Pino as Soviet agents and that these documents are in the possession of the Colombian National Police.

This, in substance, is the evidence that Fidel Castro was a Soviet agent as early as 1948. It is hard to see how the State Department could have ignored these facts if they were available to it. It is still harder to see how the Department could have informed Congress a decade later that Castro and his 26th of July Movement were free of the taint of Communism.

Yet this is precisely what happened. The basic data on Castro's conduct during the Bogotázo were in print by 1949 and available to anyone who could read Spanish. Castro was denounced as a Red by President Ospina Pérez in a 1948 radio address. The books of Alberto Niño H. and Francisco Fandiño Silva appeared in 1949. The report of Detective #6 was published in Caracas on September 22, 1949 and by *El Siglo* of Bogotá a month earlier.

One of the American officials who witnessed the Bogotázo was Roy Rubottom, secretary to the American Embassy and to the U. S. Delegation to the Inter-American Conference. The Rubottoms took care of two of Ambassador Beaulac's children during the day of slaughter and they are referred to in affectionate terms in the Ambassador's chatty book. According to *Who's Who in America* (Volume 29), Rubottom was assigned to Bogotá during 1947-49.

One might have imagined that the massive and savage display of Communist power which diplomat Rubottom lived through would have made an indelible impression on his mind. One might even have assumed that, while in Bogotá, he would have been sufficiently curious about the organization and mechanics of the uprising to read the available books and police reports and to remember the names of the principal Soviet actors in the tragedy.

This, however, was apparently not the case. In due course, Mr. Rubottom was promoted to Assistant Secretary of State for Latin American Affairs. On December 31, 1958, a day before Castro took power in Cuba, he reported to the Subcommittee for Inter-American Affairs of the Senate Foreign Relations Committee that "there was no evidence of any organized Communist element within the Castro movement or that Señor Castro himself was under Communist influence." [24]

In fact, throughout the period of Castro's rise to power and subsequent imposition of Communist rule upon Cuba, Rubottom's influence on American policy was enigmatic, if not unfortunate. On August 11, 1960, in an exclusive interview with the *Standard-Times* of New Bedford, Mass., former U. S. Ambassador to Cuba Arthur Gardner revealed that his repeated warnings that Castro was Communist-dominated were disregarded by Rubottom and his cronies. The *Standard-Times* story read:

". . . Castro became Washington's knight in shining armor and Batista, now cast in the role of villain by Rubottom and company, was being eased toward the door, and not gently.

"Nobody listened to the pleadings of America's ambassador to Cuba, who argued in vain that 'we were handling this matter in a bad and indifferent manner.'

"It was this clique that brought about Gardner's resignation from the Cuba post—because he recognized that 'Castro was no different from any other breed of Communist'—even though President Eisenhower was inclined to let Gardner serve longer."

As punishment for his insistent warnings that Castro's movement was Red-dominated and hostile to the United

[24] *New York Times*, January 1, 1959, p. 21, col. 2.

States, Ambassador Gardner was recalled in 1957. The State Department did not arrange to have the new Ambassador to Cuba, Earl E. T. Smith, talk to his predecessor, even though Gardner had the benefit of intimate knowledge of Cuban affairs and years of residence there. Gardner was never invited to come to Washington for "debriefing," a departure from precedent which can only be described as a gross and calculated insult. Instead, Rubottom and his group arranged to have Ambassador Smith briefed by *New York Times* correspondent Herbert L. Matthews, an inveterate apologist for Soviet-infiltrated movements and the American primarily responsible for the campaign of propaganda and misrepresentation which sold Fidel Castro to the people of the United States as a liberal and a democrat.

"It was primarily because of Rubottom's approval," the *Standard-Times* stated in its interview story, "that Castro was able to come to the United States in April 1959 to address the American Society of Newspaper Editors. Rubottom gave his public and private blessing to the visit and the State Department announced Castro would be 'welcomed as a distinguished leader' and would be given an official security guard 'if necessary'—even though his visit was unofficial."

At long last, on July 30, 1960, Roy Rubottom was replaced as Assistant Secretary of State for Latin American Affairs. White House press secretary James C. Hagerty announced that Rubottom would be named Ambassador to Argentina and that the transfer was not in the nature of a reprimand. This soft treatment of a man who had done perhaps irreparable damage to his country could perhaps be attributed to the fact that Rubottom had been a protégé of Milton Eisenhower, a well-intentioned, vaguely leftist former New-Deal bureaucrat who exercised massive influence over Latin American affairs chiefly because he was the President's brother.

3

Childhood and Youth of
Fidel Castro

"No, liberation and development of the individual
are not the key to our age,
they are not what our age
demands. What it needs,
what it wrestles after, what
it will create is—Terror."
—Naphta in Thomas Mann
The Magic Mountain

Fidel Castro came from a family which had money
without social position. He grew up suspended between social classes, vulnerable to insult, without strong roots, con-
scious of his murky origin and determined to force whatever
group he joined to accept him as its leader.

The formative influence of the family on Fidel Castro is
obviously crucial to his development as a revolutionary and
a man dedicated to the destruction of established social institutions. Yet, unfortunately, it is precisely in this area that
source material is scanty, often unreliable and frequently
contradictory.

Information about the childhood and youth of Fidel Castro
is contained in Jules Dubois' eulogistic and untrustworthy

biography[1] and in the naïve, but more reliable, account written by two of Fidel's sisters.[2] United Fruit Company records shed some light on the Castro family. In addition, a former brother-in-law of Fidel Castro talked to the writer as did an emigré professor who had taught at the University of Santiago de Cuba during the period when Castro attempted an insurrection there and had delved deeply into Castro's origins and background. This professor cannot be identified because he fears retaliation against close relatives incarcerated in a Castro prison. Other sources include Dr. Emilio Nuñez Portuondo, former Cuban Ambassador to the United Nations and later publisher of *Latin American Events;* the refugee Cuban writer, labor leader and former student leader, Francisco Chao Hermida; and the columnist, Drew Pearson.

Fidel Castro's father, Angel, was born in Galicia, a province in northwestern Spain. He came to the Oriente Province of Cuba in 1898 and fought against Cuban independence and against the United States Army. When the Spanish forces were defeated, Angel Castro went to work as a pick and shovel laborer for the Nipe Bay Company, a subsidiary of the United Fruit Company. On February 7, 1960, the columnist, Drew Pearson, published a story that Fidel Castro's anti-American phobia dated from his father's experiences as a supervisor at a United Fruit Company warehouse.

"The elder Castro's chief duty was to check in mule-cart-loads of sugar cane," Pearson wrote. "After seven years on that job, he was abruptly fired and charged with systematic wholesale theft of refined sugar throughout the time of his employment. The company said that Castro, in league with a warehouse guard and certain wagon drivers, would load emptied cane carts with bags of sugar and send them out to a secret storage point for subsequent contraband sale.

[1] *Fidel Castro,* Bobbs-Merrill, Indianapolis, 1959. Dubois has implicitly repudiated this book by his subsequent exposé articles on the subject of Castro and Communism.
[2] Emma y Lidia Castro as told to Michael Erice, *Vida de Fidel Castro,* nine articles published in *El Diario de Nueva York,* April 22 to May 1, 1957.

"United Fruit lawyers started prosecution against the elder Castro on these charges, but the case was eventually dropped for lack of cooperating witnesses."

The United Fruit Company investigated these charges. They were hampered by the fact that the alleged crimes of Angel Castro were committed more than half a century ago. Following the investigation, the company issued a complete denial of Pearson's account. Angel Castro never worked as a checker, was never fired, was never suspected of theft and was never prosecuted. According to United Fruit, Angel Castro worked for them building a railroad in 1904. He was a good workman and was later hired to dig ditches and put in pole bridges for sugar cane rail lines. He bought his own land with his savings as a day laborer and in 1919 or 1920 was able to sell United Fruit two or three houses which he had acquired. There are United Fruit Company employees who can recall hunting guinea hens on company land with Fidel when the latter was a boy.[3]

Following the denial of Angel Castro's employment as checker of sugar, Drew Pearson talked to his man in Havana by overseas telephone. His original source had been an American official in Santiago. Pearson checked his facts with another United States official, who has been a resident in Cuba for over thirty years, and was told that the story was correct except for the detail that United Fruit may have been shipping raw sugar, not refined, at that time. "I don't know why the United Fruit Company went out of its way to deny this story, unless it may be that they were worried over the precarious situation of their properties in Cuba and thought this might improve their position with Castro," Pearson wrote.[4]

When Angel Castro died on October 21, 1956, he left an estate worth about half a million dollars. No Cuban that this writer has talked to has ever suggested that this fortune was

---

[3] Statement of Joseph Baker of United Fruit Company to the writer, May 16, 1960.
[4] Letter from Drew Pearson to the writer, May 20, 1960.

acquired by honest toil, either as a day laborer or as a sugar farmer and rural businessman.

According to Dr. Nuñez Portuondo, Angel Castro laid the foundations of his estate by putting himself at the head of a group of militia during the 1917 civil war in Oriente Province. He took land belonging to supporters of the liberal cause and added them to his own holdings.[5] Later, he acquired more land by moving the fences on American-owned absentee properties and by squatting on other people's land and planting cane on it. Castro, Sr., was involved almost continuously in lawsuits brought by outraged landowners and others who claimed he had defrauded them.

By the time he was in his early teens, the elder Castro and Fidel's mother had decided to have Fidel trained as a lawyer so he could protect the family property against these attacks. "At this period, our mother was full of advice," wrote Emma and Lidia Castro. " 'Fidel,' she told him, 'you must study and be diligent. And with all the talking you do, some day you will manage to become a lawyer!' "[6]

In his youth, Angel Castro married a Cuban woman who had been a schoolteacher. By her, he had two children, Lidia and Pedro Emilio. Later, he had an established liaison with the cook in the household, Lina Ruz Gonzales. She bore him five children, among them Ramon, Fidel, Raul and Emma. Since Angel Castro was a Catholic, he was unable to marry Fidel's mother until the death of his first wife.

This situation obviously contributed to the atmosphere of tension and mutual hatred characteristic of the family. The two children by the first wife resented the fact that a former servant was mistress of the house. For Fidel, it meant carrying the stigma of illegitimacy and, to that extent, being an outsider in terms of Cuban society.[7]

[5] Statement made to the writer, December 22, 1959.
[6] Emma y Lidia Castro, *op. cit.*
[7] According to Dr. Nuñez Portuondo, the Castros were people with no family feeling. They disliked each other; they never got along with their father and hardly ever saw him.

In the 1940's, Pedro Emilio Castro, the son by the first wife, fell out with his father because the latter refused to give him the money he wanted for an electoral campaign. Consequently, Pedro Emilio denounced the elder Castro in a series of diatribes over the radio in Santiago de Cuba, which were later published in a local newspaper.

The son went into sordid detail about the ways in which his father had acquired land. He also charged him with murdering workers and with being an active supporter of the Nazi movement in Cuba.

People who knew the Castro family well during Fidel's childhood and youth back the first story without reservation. They state it is common knowledge that the Castro couple ruled their largely Negro cane choppers by gun law, that they killed workmen who stepped too far out of line, that husband and wife never went into the fields without their gun belts and that the local military post, consisting of a corporal and two soldiers, slept on Castro land, ate Castro food and received a small Castro stipend.

As the years passed, Angel Castro became increasingly unable to manage his property, both because of advancing age and drunkenness. His fears increased and he got into the habit of protecting himself against assassination by sleeping outside the house and in a different place every night. (This is a practice which his son, Fidel, would follow for exactly the same reason after taking power in Cuba.)

One of the brothers of Fidel Castro's divorced wife, who was one of Fidel's closest friends at the University of Havana, visited him at his family place in Biran in the northern part of Oriente. He was amazed that a family worth half a million dollars should live like savages. There was a large ramshackle house, but no toilet, merely an outhouse. Fidel's friend was impressed at the lack of any family life. As he told the story, when one of the Castro's felt hungry, he would go to the kitchen, cut off a chunk of beef and fry it. He would eat in the kitchen or on his way to the fields. The guest could remember no occasion on which the whole family shared a meal. The Castro children seemed united by no common bond.

There were no books in the house. Poultry wandered through the kitchen. The mother of the second brood of children was hard, resourceful and exceptionally competent. She ran the sugar plantation, the general store and the sugar mill. It is clear from the reminiscences of the two Castro sisters that the mother was the dominant force in the family, that she believed in education for her children and had high ambitions for them.

Angel Castro was an aloof man who seldom spoke to his children. While he was financially generous to them, he was in frequent conflict with Fidel. The first known manifestation of this conflict occurred when Fidel was about thirteen. He had fallen under the strong political influence of a Spanish Communist and veteran of the Spanish Civil War who was a worker for Angel Castro. Characteristically, Fidel reacted to ideas with action and organized a strike of his father's workers. The elder Castro was outraged. He considered having his son imprisoned, but was told that Fidel had violated no law.

Parental opposition is evident in the biography prepared by Emma and Lidia Castro. The admiring sisters try to gloss over the conflict and make it appear to be merely an expression of Fidel's sense of social injustice. In the first of their nine articles, Emma and Lidia state that Fidel told them, when he was still young enough to go about barefoot, that the land belonged to the people and not to landlords like their father. The second article describes another clash:

"One day, when papa reproached him in our house, *with mama's consent*,[8] Fidel, who was then eighteen and like many other boys of that age considered himself a mature man, replied:

" 'I am in the University studying law and this same study

[8] My emphasis—N.W.

of the law makes me defend what is right—even with naked hands. I defend the rights of the oppressed poor against those who abuse the powers they wrenched from the people with deceitful promises; that is my battle.' "

To dismiss these explosions of protest as Oedipal manifestations or as merely the effect of Communist propaganda on an immature mind would do violence to the truth. There were real social evils in Cuba. Ostentatious wealth, often corruptly acquired and irresponsibly wasted, coexisted with grinding poverty in the countryside during the period of Castro's youth. A large part of the Cuban upper class was lacking in social responsibility or a conception of *noblesse oblige*. The situation was not improved by the fact that a considerable part of the wealth of the island was in the hands of people who had been shaken up from the lower strata of the social order in the course of the struggle for independence and the spasms of local disorder and civil war that followed it. On the other hand, Cuba had very advanced labor and social welfare legislation; the working-class, particularly in the cities, was steadily increasing its share of the national income; health and education were improving and the Cuban masses were considerably better off than the majority of Latin Americans. In short, the nation seemed to have moved from chaos to order and was making orderly progress toward better living conditions for its people.

In the Oriente, and particularly in its rural regions, the social evils against which Fidel Castro protested were considerably more glaring than elsewhere on the island. The province was remote from the capital; it was an area of recent sugar cane expansion and hence of *nouveaux riches* planters; the fact that the working masses were mainly Negroes, many of them immigrants from Haiti, piled racial stress on economic conflict. And at Biran, his father's property, Fidel saw rapacity, theft, embezzlement and even murder in microcosm. At Biran, families of workers were huddled in one-room thatched shacks with dirt floors and open fires for cooking. There were no doctors or dentists. Children worked hauling water and picking coffee beans from the age of five. If they had shoes, they were castoffs donated by the Castro family.[9]

Years later, in 1941 Fidel Castro would remember Biran and start "a campaign against the system of forced labor inflicted on soldiers in the private farms and plantations of high civilian and military officials, providing facts, photographs, films and proofs of every sort, which he submitted to the courts in denouncing these practices on March 3, (1952)."[10]

To revert to Castro's boyhood. After he had organized the strike, his father shipped him out of Biran, enrolling him as a boarder in the Colegio Dolores in Santiago de Cuba. This was a Jesuit institution which taught orthodox principles and doctrines which met with the elder Castro's approval.

Fidel was accepted in the fairly exclusive society of Santiago by his schoolmates, but he wanted more. He made a bid for leadership of the student body, but was rebuffed. When he became insistent, he was told that this was impossible because he was a bastard.

After Dolores, he was sent to the Colegio Belen in Havana, another Jesuit institution. At this point, the up-to-now barely discernible shoots of rebelliousness, hatred of authority and smouldering violence begin to assume significant proportions. First, a minor episode, included in their naïvely eulogistic articles by the Castro sisters: "When he was studying, Fidel tore out the pages of his books and threw them away . . . to make an impression on everybody."

When he was about fifteen, Fidel made another and much more desperate bid to gain recognition and leadership. He

---

[9] Ray Brennan, *Castro, Cuba and Justice,* Doubleday & Co., Garden City, 1959, pp. 32-3. While this book is pro-Castro propaganda, its description of conditions at Biran checks with other sources.
[10] Emma and Lidia Castro, *op. cit.,* fourth article.

bet that he could ride his bicycle at top speed into a stone or concrete pillar. He did so and was unconscious for days.

A year later, he argued with a teacher about his grades. He stormed out of the building, got a pistol and returned with the intention of finding and killing the offender. The teacher, however, had been warned and had fled. Friends managed to calm Fidel and take his gun away from him.

According to the official records, he was an excellent athlete, a good student in literary subjects and an enthusiastic debater. The Colegio Belen Yearbook for 1945 predicted that his life would be filled with "brilliant pages" and added that "the actor in him will not be lacking." [11] This is the official story. The unofficial one is that he was a mediocre student, who managed to finish in three years instead of the usual four by bribing or threatening his professors and by getting those who were Communists or Communist sympathizers to give him passing grades gratis.

The episode of the bicycle has intrigued several Cuban exiles who know about it. Did Fidel Castro suffer brain damage as a result? There is some reason to suspect this. As a mature man, he is afflicted with logorrhea, a psychopathological condition defined in *Webster's New International Dictionary*, 2nd edition, as "excessive and often incoherent talkativeness." There have been occasions when Fidel Castro became so unintelligible during one of this three-to-five-hour harangues that he had to be pulled away from the microphone by aides. When this occurred, he would submit with docility and seem to be in a dazed state. People who know him well report that he sometimes has momentary fainting spells suggestive of *petit mal* epilepsy.[12]

[11] Quoted in Dubois, *op. cit.*, p. 15.
[12] "In the idiopathic form of epilepsy, the two factors which appear to be responsible for the condition are first, an inherited instability of cortical neurones and, secondly some factor which determines the appearance of fits, such as trauma or infection." Geoffrey Evans, M.D., F.R.C.P., *Medical Treatment: Principles and their Application*, Butterworth and Co., London, 1951, pp. 281-2.

The abnormal behavior of Fidel Castro was partially matched by that of his father and his half brother, Pedro Emilio. Fidel grew up in a family rent by hostility and jealousy. He was in conflict with a father who was a drunkard, a swindler and a killer, a man so cowardly he was afraid to sleep in his own house. There was the burden of being illegitimate, the vulnerability to insult and the overwhelming need, never gratified, to be applauded and followed as a leader. Thus, by the time Fidel Castro reached young manhood, psychological, and possibly physically traumatic, forces had shaped his character so as to make him receptive to the destructive career that he would embark upon.

4

The Student Assassins

"The revolutionary enters
the world of the state, of
the classes and of so-called
civilization, and he lives in
this world only because he
has faith in its quick and
complete destruction. He
no longer remains a revolutionary if he keeps faith
with anything in this world.
*He should not hesitate to
destroy any position, any
place or any man in this
world.*[1] He must hate everything and everyone with
an equal hatred. All the
worse for him if he has
in the world relationships
with parents, friends, or
lovers; *he is no longer a revolutionary if he is swayed
by these relationships.*"

—Sergei Gennadiyevich
Nechayev
*The Revolutionary
Catechism*[2]

[1] Emphasis in the original.
[2] Translated by Robert Payne, from *Zero*, John Day, New York, 1950, pp.
10-11.

Fidel Castro entered the University of Havana in 1945 at the age of nineteen. Here he attracted attention because of his unusual height and powerful physique, his driving, aggressive personality and his tendency to try to overpower all opposition with a torrent of words. In high school, Fidel had starred as a basketball player and had become accustomed to applause. At the University, he was not outstanding enough to make a great impression. He threw himself enthusiastically into debating, an ideal area for a histrionic character thirsting for leadership. Castro's debating style consisted of piling one dogmatic assertion on another. It was weak in logic and thus he was never able to win first prize. This rankled, and, in speaking to friends, he attributed his failure to bias and persecution on the part of the judges.

While he was not popular with most of the students, Fidel Castro attracted a group of satellites. For the most part, his followers were undersized and undistinguished in appearance. They were socially unacceptable and resentful. Fidel easily dominated them and towered over them physically.

The Cult of Uncleanliness

Fidel Castro had an allowance of $200 a month from his father, more than adequate in the mid-1940's. Yet he wore dirty and old clothes, seldom bathed or bothered to change his shirt, ignored the barbershop and was ostentatious about appearing bohemian and unwashed. This and his uncouth manners contributed to his unpopularity with the student body. His nickname at the University was *bola de churre*, which means *ball of dirty grease*.

Patria, a Miami Cuban refugee paper, published in its March 15, 1960 issue a photograph of Fidel Castro, the

University student, fingering his stockinged feet. The article
below the photograph read in part:

"This is the Fidel whom nobody remembers. The one
with the ugly and dirty habit of taking off his shoes everywhere. With sweating feet and patched and torn socks. Always touching them. And afterwards bringing his hands to
his mouth. They were as filthy as his feet.

"This is the Fidel whom students at the University treated
as a grease ball, without any respect whatsoever. And whom
the majority of the students scrupulously avoided."

The assertion that Fidel was known at the University as
bola de churre does not rest solely on the authority of a
sometimes strident emigré press. The nickname and the reasons for it have been corroborated by several Cubans, including a former Havana University professor, who is one of
the most eminent and, incidentally, one of the most leftwing of Castro's opponents. This man refuses to be quoted
on this particular matter because he believes that any public
statement concerning Fidel Castro's personal peculiarities
and vices would weaken the effectiveness of his political opposition to the regime.

The filthy personal habits of Fidel Castro, the student,
were neither accidental nor unimportant; they would be repeated on a more grandiose scale by his 26th of July Movement; in fact, being unwashed and unshaven would be the
badge by which the revolutionary *barbudos* would be known
to the Cuban people and the world.

The cultivation of personal uncleanliness symbolizes a desire to defile on a much larger scale. An anonymous leaflet
in Spanish of unknown date or provenance observes with
considerable insight that "the frustrations in the private and
public life of this son of the Spanish immigrant, Angel Castro (a notorious stealer of livestock and geophage[3])" made

---

[3] A geophage is an earth eater. In Spanish, this does not refer to the starving
creatures who eat soil to fill their empty bellies, but to those who devour land
belonging to others.

him "react in an enraged fashion against the traditional institutions of the society in which he was allowed to live." The leaflet adds: "Undoubtedly, Fidel Castro, alias *bola de churre*, showed from his first years in school that he suffered from a complex because of his unfortunate and inferior origin."

The significance of grime and dirt as the emblem of a political movement is greater in the Spanish and Ibero-American culture than in other milieux. Francisco Chao Hermida, an expert on the psychiatry of revolution and terror, observed the first months of the victorious Castro revolution in Cuba. "The Cuban man," he wrote, "is affectedly nice as to dress, proud of being well-clothed and personally clean." Beards, even for old men, were virtually unknown in Cuba. For one thing, the climate does not make them desirable.

"Good. Then one day the bearded ones triumphed, grimy and stinking. It was quite something to see how the most beautifully groomed young ladies switched over to them and how the victors availed themselves of the most exclusive places in the company of people who 48 hours earlier would have given them alms as beggars . . . From then on filthiness and the habit of not washing became the tone of legitimate revolutionary pride. Letting one's beard grow, not bathing, were means of identifying with the revolution. Thus, a species of brain washing began which will radically transform the soul and mentality of Cuba." [4]

In Chao Hermida's opinion, the chief objective of the cult of uncleanliness is to destroy the family and the home. As he sees it, the women's militia of the Spanish Loyalists played a very similar role. There was an honorable tradition of woman partisans, springing from the Spanish popular risings against Napoleonic role, but in the Communist version 120 years later, la Pasionaria[5] was publicized as the

[4] Francisco Chao Hermida, *Un Año Despues,* Mexico City, December 1959, pp. 10-11.
[5] Dolores Ibarruri.

leader of these Amazons and "presented as the ideal of Spanish womanhood." When he characterizes la Pasionaria as "a vulgar prostitute," Chao Hermida may be exaggerating slightly. But it is quite true that she was "one of the most despicable and self-seeking careerists of the Communist movement" [6] and that, after the defeat of the Loyalist forces, she waged a veritable campaign of extermination from the safe haven of the Soviet Union against the more decent and honorable leaders of Spanish Communism. "Shortly after the Republic was crushed by fascism and Red betrayal," Chao Hermida writes, "la Pasionaria declared that she had a legion of children and that her greatest pride was that she did not know who was the father of any of them." [7]

The cult of dirt was by no means confined to Loyalist Spain or Castro's Cuba. Historically, filth has been exalted as a virtue by certain religious groups, which wished to convince their disciples that they should turn their backs on the world, and by those secular revolutionary movements which were determined to inculcate hatred of the institutions, values and achievements of the prevailing social order. In the latter case, the cult of dirt is suppressed once the revolution passes its destructive and nihilist phase and the revolutionary bureaucracy creates new institutions and vested interests which it is determined to defend.

The Environment of Terror

During the years that Fidel Castro was enrolled in Havana University, a special environment of terrorism poisoned the air. To understand the historic roots of this situation, one has to make a detour into recent Cuban history.

In 1925, General Gerardo Machado y Morales was elected President of Cuba with Liberal support. This man has been

[6] Franz Borkenau, *European Communism*, Faber & Faber, London 1953, p. 164. For more sordid details concerning la Pasionaria, see Enrique Castro Delgado, *J'ai perdu ma foi à Moscou*, Paris, 1950.
[7] Chao Hermida, *op. cit.*, p. 11.

customarily portrayed as a Caribbean Hitler and a monster
with an insatiable thirst for blood. Actually, he was a greedy
and unscrupulous politician of exceptional shrewdness,
who built the most powerful political machine in the history
of the island. Although he promised not to seek re-election,
he extended the presidential term, built up the army and
ruled by a combination of graft, manipulation and naked
power.

Machado made the mistake of suppressing all opposition.
Accordingly, the ABC Revolutionary Organization, a secret
terrorist group, was founded in December 1931.[8] It was characteristic of the anonymity and nihilism of this movement
that the letters ABC stood for nothing at all.

Students in the University of Havana and elsewhere
played a leading role in the fierce, subterranean struggle
which followed. The secret police of Machado, the *Porra*,
tortured and butchered students. The ABC retaliated with
bomb outrages in which dozens of innocent bystanders were
killed, and with political assassinations. As the world depres-
sion gathered momentum, discontent spread and the power
of the ABC grew. In 1932-33, the writer negotiated with
ABC terrorist leaders in New York City concerning the terms
and conditions under which the National Student League,
the Communist-dominated organization of American college
students, would support their battle. The Cuban leaders in
these negotiations seemed to be of upper class and professional origin. They were impressive because of their physical beauty, their evident intrepidity and the exaltation and
tension which they communicated. As political negotiators,
they seemed inflexible, sectarian and unable to grasp the
fundamentals of public relations.

[8] The evolution of Machado and the ABC is taken chiefly from *Cuba: Island
of Paradox*, McDowell, Obolensky, New York, 1959, by Ruby Hart Phillips,
the Cuban correspondent of the New York *Times*. This excellent political
analysis is marred by a romanticized treatment of Fidel Castro and his movement, which no longer reflects Mrs. Phillips' attitude.

Under the pressures imposed by the newly elected Franklin D. Roosevelt administration, Machado was forced out in the summer of 1933. Shortly thereafter, Dr. Grau San Martin, a professor of medicine at Havana University and a leading figure in the terrorist struggles against Machado, was named President of Cuba by the Student Directory. This tall, anemic visionary lacked executive ability, tact or the capacity to restore order. He spent his time ranting against American capitalism and in interminable meetings with the leaders of the Student Directory, who were totally untrained in the business of government.

As chaos intensified, Sergeant Fulgencio Batista seized power in a coup d'etat. Batista was not a military leader, nor was he a fascist, a reactionary, or a man avid for power. He was a male stenographer who wore a uniform because he was employed by, and a member of, the Cuban Army. He came from very humble origins. As a boy, he had found it hard to get enough to eat, and his brother had died of tuberculosis aggravated by inadequate nutrition and lack of medical care.[9] Hence, Batista was strongly pro-labor and favored advanced, and perhaps in the Cuban situation impractical, social welfare legislation.

Nor did he want to be a dictator. As Ruby Hart Phillips points out,[10] Batista and his conspirators were not only willing, but anxious, to turn over the power they had seized to those senior officers of the Cuban Army who had clean records and reputations. They feared that the alternative would be American intervention under the Platt Amendment.[11] Through a series of amazing and incomprehensible misun-

[9] Austin F. MacDonald, *Latin American Politics and Government*, Thomas Y. Crowell, New York, 1949, p. 539.
[10] *Op. cit.*, pp. 87-94.
[11] Drafted by Senator Thomas Platt in 1904, this amendment provided that United States forces had the right to intervene in Cuba whenever necessary. The Platt Amendment was eventually incorporated in the Cuban Constitution, but was abrogated, many Cubans think, unwisely, by President Roosevelt in early 1934.

derstandings, President Roosevelt's special representative in Cuba, Sumner Welles, conveyed the impression that the United States was about to intervene militarily to overthrow the Batista regime. Under these circumstances, the senior officers naturally refused to accept office from Batista's hands. Since no United States intervention occurred, Batista found himself the strong man of Cuba.

In 1940, he ran for office, as the coalition candidate of a group of parties, which included the Communist Party, and was elected. He was thirty-nine at the time and had already been the real power in Cuba for seven years.

In 1944, Batista surprised both his friends and his enemies by permitting free elections. As a result, his candidate was defeated by the popular idol and standard bearer of the Republican Authentic Alliance (*Autenticos*), Dr. Ramon Grau San Martin. The victory of Grau was the occasion for three days of wild celebrations. The new President immediately boasted that he would make Cuba "economically independent" of the United States, an economic absurdity. He proceeded to pile additional taxes on the Cuban people so that he could pay out doles to politically powerful pressure groups. One of his strokes of economic statesmanship was to levy a tax on toothpaste to pay for pensions for retired dentists. The new President pledged a lavish program of public works, but the funds were embezzled and all that was done was to pave a few streets in Havana.

"It is not I who have taken office today, but the people," Grau declared when inaugurated. When he retired from office, he was credited with having stolen more money from the people than any other Cuban political leader, a singular achievement. Grau's successor, President Antonio Prio Socarrás, also an *Autentico* leader, had him haled before the Audiencia Court of Havana to answer charges that he and his cronies had misappropriated $174,000,000. Grau pleaded not guilty. On July 4, 1950, a group of gunmen invaded the courts and stole the documents that might have convicted him. Nobody was ever arrested for this theft and none of the pilfered documents were ever recovered.[12]

In his second term of office, 1952-58, Fulgencio Batista would steal tens of millions of dollars. His enemies claim that he embezzled more than the light-fingered professor.[13] The difference was that Batista stole and built, whereas Grau stole and wrecked.

Grau San Martin had been the candidate of the terrorist and revolutionary organizations. These emerged from the underground to participate in his campaign and direct his strategy. "After the inauguration," wrote Ruby Hart Phillips, "these groups, particularly the nine most powerful organizations, moved in on various government ministries. In time they became almost an invisible government, imposing their decisions on cabinet ministers, government officials and sometimes even the President himself." [14]

When Grau welched on his pledge to pardon several imprisoned revolutionaries, the terrorists blamed the Chief of the Secret Service, Enrique Enriquez. They killed him with machine-gun fire. "Crime was becoming widespread in all parts of the island and the police seemed powerless to cope with it," Austin MacDonald wrote in his *Latin American Politics and Government*, "In two years there were nearly fifty political murders. Graft was as common as it had ever been in the history of the nation." [15] The main reason Cuba was able to stand these intolerable abuses was that she was riding high on the inflated raw materials prices of the immediate postwar period.

When Fidel Castro entered Havana University in 1945, he was in the maelstrom of a morally corrupt situation, which particularly affected university students. Disillusionment with constructive purpose was coupled with the habit-

[12] Phillips, *op. cit.*, pp. 253-4.
[13] A former United States Ambassador to Cuba estimated in a conversation with the writer that Batista's take was $40,000,000.
[14] *op. cit.*, p. 231.
[15] *op. cit.*, p. 543.

ual and unrestrained resort to violence. The causes have already been indicated. The revolutionary terrorists who overthrew the Machado regime may have been heroes of the mob, but they had no valid program for their country. In office, these men denounced Wall Street, inveighed against American imperialism, pandered to the extreme nationalism of the Cuban masses, favored labor and social welfare measures, regardless of the carrying capacity of the economy, and frequently handicapped any healthy economic expansion.

The morale of the Cuban Army had been shattered by Batista's successful coup d'etat and by his inability to transfer the hot potato of military power to more legitimate hands. An officer corps which had been kicked out by a conspiracy of non-coms was neither obeyed nor respected. The new officers included the successful conspirators of the Batista putsch. For the most part, they had displayed no military abilities or grasp of military science. They had not been trained in the officer's code of conduct nor seasoned in battle. It should be recalled that the sergeants' conspiracy which brought Batista to power was revolution by switchboard, that is to say, the key men were the non-commissioned officers responsible for telephone communications in the key forts, camps and barracks. The country being near chaos and the legitimate military leadership bewildered by the fall of Machado, all Batista had to do was plot by telephone, then move troops toward bloodless victory.

The leftwing administrations which followed Batista shook up the high commands of the Army and police, promoting men to the highest positions who could be trusted not to betray them. This meant that partisan political activity, and for that matter conspiracy, were the most effective roads to promotion and power in those organizations of the state which wielded physical force. Of course, there were honorable and dedicated career officers in the Cuban armed forces, men thoroughly trained in their profession, but the military and police environment in which they sought to function had been corrupted.

The terrorists were hungry for loaves and fishes and one of the many organizations they penetrated at a high bureaucratic level was the national police. Divided among a dozen or so organizations, they were always in competition and sometimes at each other's throats. The older terrorists and revolutionaries recruited younger men. Under the Grau San Martin regime, with the terrorists in high positions of political power and free to commit political murders with virtual impunity, such recruitment was easy.

One of the chief leaders of student terrorists at the University of Havana in Fidel Castro's time had this to say about the sequential stages of moral decay: "Under Machado, terrorism was justified on the theory that it is necessary to kill the machine whichs kills. When Machado was removed, the terrorist organizations survived. Like other politically active groups in Cuba, they became poisoned by the amorality of Marxism-Leninism. At first, they used the pretext of irreconcilable political differences to justify killing. Then they killed to settle conflicting claims for power. In the end, 'we killed in order not to be killed.' "

The terrorist organizations were essentially alliances between student revolutionary groups and warring factions within a national police department which had been staffed by the victorious insurrectionaries who had overthrown Machado. Trade union activists were also in the terrorist bands, for the unions were closely tied to the governmental political machine; strikes were won because of government intervention; trade union offices, with ample opportunities for gain, were often handed out to politicians and particularly to the leaders of the nine major underground revolutionary groups backing the Grau administration.

The terrorists did not kill people to determine elections. They could not be equated to American gangsters since they never killed for money. They denied that they found killing exhilarating. This mode of political action appealed to the romantic characteristics of young intellectuals bred in the Hispanic tradition, a culture which has sometimes been described as death-obsessed. There is a certain analogy between terrorist and toreador for in both cases the hero proves his manhood by playing with death.

5

Apprenticeship in Murder

> "Happiness lies only in that
> which excites and the only
> thing that excites is crime."
> —the Marquis de Sade

AT THE University of Havana, Fidel Castro's closest friend was Rafael Diaz Balart, a young man who also
hailed from Oriente Province and whose family was prominent in Cuban national politics. Diaz Balart introduced Fidel
to his sister, Mirtha; they fell in love and in 1948 were married. In succeeding years, the relationship became very
strained because of Diaz Balart's opposition to Castro's Communist associations and activities. Diaz Balart proceeded to
the United States, where he organized an underground group
called the White Rose, dedicated to the revolutionary overthrow of the Castro regime.

On May 3, 1960, Rafael Diaz Balart testified before the
Senate Internal Security Subcommittee, covering, among
other subjects, the murders in which Fidel Castro was implicated while a student at Havana University. He was asked
specifically about Leonel Gomez, the president of the student body at Havana High School No. 1, who was shot in
the lungs, but not fatally, in 1947 on Ronda Street in Havana.

61

Q: Do you know who shot him?

A: Yes, sir. Fidel Castro.

Q: How do you know this?

A: Because Fidel Castro told me that. He invited me to participate with him in the killing of that student and I refused because I am a Christian. I am against killing and, besides that, there was not any reason to.

Q: Why did he want to kill Gomez?

A: Because he thought at that moment that Gomez, being a personal friend of President Grau San Martin, at that moment the President of Cuba, he was going to be a big obstacle before the ambition of Castro.

Q: Was Gomez a Communist?

A: No, I do not think so.

Q: Was he an anti-Communist?

A: I think so.

Q: Was Castro in your home immediately after the shooting of Gomez?

A: Yes, sir.

Q: What was he doing there?

A: He was trying to hide.

Q: He was there by your invitation?

A: No, he was there because he was my friend.

Q: Did you know Manolo Castro?

A: Yes . . . He was the leader and President of the Federation of University Students of Havana University, a great leader of the student body.

Q: Is he alive?

A: No, he was killed by Castro.

Q: Personally?

A: I think so.

Q: How did he kill him?

A: It was in the middle of a street in Havana. There was very much publicized by all the papers in Havana. And Castro before, some weeks before, had told publicly in Havana University, that he was going to kill Manolo Castro.

Diaz Balart proceeded to explain that he was not in Havana at the time of the murder of Manolo Castro and therefore was not speaking from his personal knowledge. The questioning proceeded:

Q: Do you know Fernandez Caral?

A: Yes, he was sergeant of the police body at Havana University.

Q: Is he still alive?

A: No, he was killed by Fidel Castro.

Q: How do you know this?

A: Because Fidel Castro had told to all my friends after he killed (Manolo) Castro that he was going to have to kill Fernandez Caral, because the sergeant had told him that he was going to put Fidel in jail because of the previous killing.

Q: Do you have any personal knowledge respecting the killing of Caral?

A: No, through my brothers, and through the other friend—I was not in Havana.

Another source is a typewritten report in my possession, "Origin and Establishment of the Communist Party in the Republic of Cuba," prepared by an officer of the Bureau for the Repression of Communist Activities (BRAC).[1] This document states that Fidel Castro Ruz "had participated in person in the death or assassination of Manolo Castro on San Rafael Street in front of 'Cinecito,' and had also participated in person in the assault on Sgt. Fernando Caral of the University Police (Guards); had been fighting in 1947 to overthrow Trujillo, had been arrested for that crime, and, in addition, had a criminal record of student street fighting."

The dossier of the Cuban national police on Fidel Alejandro Castro Ruz, after describing him as white, 32 years old, married, a lawyer, 6 feet tall, 178 pounds, literate, residing at 1352-23rd Street and with finger print card 128-587, proceeds as follows:

---

[1] This will be referred to hereafter as BRAC Report.

"A member of the illegal terrorist organization called the 'Insurrectionary and Revolutionary Union' . . .

"22 January 1948. On the night of the day in question and at the corner of San Rafael and Consulado Streets, in front of the 'Resumen' cinema theatre, the ex-President of the University Student Federation, Manolo Castro Campos, and Carlos Pucho Samper were killed by gun fire. Fidel Castro Ruz was named as the intellectual author of the crime and was arrested on the 26th of the same month when walking along San Lazaro Street in front of Maceo Park."

The police report had this to say about the murder of Sgt. Fernandez Caral:

"4 July 1948. Fidel Castro Ruz, having been identified as one of the authors of the death by bullet wounds of Sergeant Oscar Fernandez Caral of the University police, was arrested and charged on the following day. (There is no record of any indictment or trial.)"

So much for the documentation. The story behind these assaults and murders reveals the emerging psychopathic personality of the future dictator of Cuba. In 1945-46, Fidel Castro told Rafael Diaz Balart that he planned to get himself elected president of the student body of the University. The next stepping stone would be head of the Cuban Federation of University Students. This in turn would give him enough leverage for the revolutionary overthrow of the Grau San Martin regime. This plan was pure power politics and revealed the hypocrisy of the pose Fidel Castro would later strike as the champion of democracy and foe of Batista dictatorship. Corrupt and incompetent as it was, the Grau government had been chosen by the people of Cuba in as fair an election as the island had ever held. In addition, the plan was wholly unrealistic. The University of Havana had 13,000 students. Fidel Castro was in his first year there. He was unknown to most of the students and unpopular, because of his radicalism and slovenly habits, with most of those who did know him.

It was in pursuit of this plan that he proposed to Diaz Balart that they kill Leonel Gomez. Fidel made it quite clear that he had nothing against Gomez personally and in fact didn't even know him. Gomez had to be liquidated for the simple reason that he was a close friend and protégé of President Grau. Therefore, it was certain that he would be pushed into the leadership of the Havana University students as soon as he arrived there. He was a stumbling block to Fidel's ambitions.

Turned down by Diaz Balart, Castro took two members of the Rolando Masferrer gang, of which he was then a member, and lay in wait for Leonel Gomez outside the university stadium where Gomez was watching a football game. Fidel opened fire on Gomez and wounded him in the lung. His two companions took no part in the gun fight.

When he realized that Gomez had walked away from the ambush, Fidel Castro panicked. He knew that Leonel Gomez had been prominent in the UIR (Insurrectionary Revolutionary Union), the leading luminary of which was Police Major Emilio Tró, described by his enemies as a psychopathic assassin who killed for fun, but regarded by his followers as a leader of outstanding courage. Fidel Castro heard that Major Tró was planning to have him shot in revenge for the Gomez attack.

The terrified Castro reached a swift decision. He was afraid to face Major Tró personally, but he sent an intermediary to apologize for the assault, allege that Fidel had been merely a catspaw of the real organizer of the affair, Chief of Secret Police Major Mario Salabarrios (who had in fact been implicated), and propose that Fidel Castro shift allegiance from Masferrer's gang to Tró's. This sordid offer of betrayal was accepted and it saved Fidel Castro's life.

Immediately after the attempted murder, Fidel Castro had hidden out at the house of General Juan Rodriguez, an exile from the Dominican Republic who was hatching a plot to invade Trujillo's realm from Cuban soil. Castro hit it off excellently with this veteran Dominican politician and half-educated cattleman. As a result, the blustering, gun-toting law student interrupted his career as an academic gangster long enough to join the Cayo Confites expedition that was supposed to invade the Dominican Republic and liberate its subjects.

This operation had the tacit support of the Grau San Martin government. About 1,500 Cubans, Dominicans, Venezuelans, Guatemalans and other Latin Americans, comprising what would later be known as the Caribbean Legion, were trained, largely by Communist veterans of the Spanish Civil War, at Cayo Confites while $2,000,000 of arms was assembled at the finca, *America*, of the Cuban Minister of Education, José Aleman. The money spent in this operation was misappropriated from Ministry of Education funds, evidently with the knowledge and consent of President Grau.

The armada consisted of two ships, twelve to fourteen planes, artillery, bazookas, hundreds of rifles and machine guns. This materiel was bought in the United States as war surplus and assembled in Cuban ports. The planes were landed on Cuban airfields. The conspiracy was an open secret.

The operation was heavily infiltrated by Communists and to a very large extent under Communist leadership. "My research in Cuba in the summer of 1948 established clearly that the Communists were participating in these activities," Professor William S. Stokes reported.[2] After the Cayo Confites affair, the Organization of American States investigated the Caribbean Legion. Dr. Enrique Corominas, the President of the Commission, pointed out that the organization was "more offensive than defensive" and that, while it alleged it was fighting for democracy and freedom, "the regimes that have supported the formation of mercenary

[2] Printed in *Soviet Total War*, U. S. House of Representatives, Document #227, Part 2.

troops to attack other countries have not been characterized by liberal and democratic practices." Without mentioning Communism, specifically, Corominas noted that the Legion was "an international revolutionary force" and "a threat to the tranquility of the countries of Central America and the Caribbean."

The chief agent of Minister Aleman in arms buying and smuggling was a young man named Manolo Castro, previously mentioned. No relation to Fidel, Manolo Castro was Sports Director of Cuba, a former President of the Student Federation of Havana University and co-director with Rolando Masferrer of the dominant political organization in the University, the Socialist Revolutionary Movement (MSR). Like other student leaders, Manolo Castro had a police record. He had been accused of murdering a professor of architecture at Havana University.

At Miami, Manolo Castro established headquarters in a large hotel, bought arms right and left with a bare minimum of conspiratorial precautions, boasted of his importance as a key revolutionary leader and behaved with such appalling indiscretion that the *Miami Herald* exposed the invasion plans. Caught in a spotlight of publicity, the State Department felt compelled to bring pressure on the Cuban Government to prevent the invasion. Manolo Castro was caught trying to smuggle two tons of small arms by plane from Florida to the Cuban insurrectionary force. He was arrested and indicted in a Florida court, but skipped bail to his native country.

Meanwhile, the invasion force trained, and turned to bronze in the sweltering Cuban summer sun. It suffered from lack of food and water due to wretched logistic planning. As the weeks dragged on, desertions increased. As United States pressure mounted, Grau finally acted. The elements at Cayo Confites were surrounded by Cuban troops and their seaward escape was blocked by the Cuban fleet. Eleven planes and 1,150 volunteers were seized.

At Cayo Confites, Rolando Masferrer reduced Fidel Castro to the ranks. "You might say that I was Fidel's tutor," he told newspapermen Martin and Santora. "In 1947, I organized an expedition against Trujillo and the Dominican Republic. Castro was one of the men I helped train. Even then he had a bad temper, was insolent, arrogant and intolerant. He was so bad for morale I had to remove him from command of a platoon." [3]

Castro was not among the Cayo Confites men taken prisoner. The official story, as narrated by Jules Dubois, is that "Fidel Castro, aboard one of the landing craft, was not going to let himself get caught—a trait that was to be exercised on many occasions—and accordingly jumped overboard with his submachine gun. Despite the drag of the gun, he managed to swim ashore." [4] The two Castro sisters have their brother under arrest and hence disarmed in a barge which was taking him to prison. Fidel jumped overboard, they state, and swam through shark-infested waters to freedom. Ruby Hart Phillips[5] also brings sharks into the scene and adds to the heroism of her subject by transforming Castro's submachine gun into a machine gun and ammunition belt.

Cuban exiles who are familiar with these events do not question Fidel Castro's abilities as a swimmer. They suggest, however, that the reason for the swim was not so much love of liberty as the fact that he was pushed overboard either by Masferrer or by one of his henchmen.

The Cayo Confites fiasco brought disgrace to Minister of Education Aleman and forced his resignation from the Cabinet. He died in Miami several years later, leaving an estate of several millions acquired as a Cuban public servant.

Back at the University, Fidel Castro again plunged into

---

[3] Joseph Martin and Phil Santora, *The Real Castro,* 7th article of the series, *New York Daily News,* March-April, 1960.
[4] *op. cit.,* p. 17.   [5] *op. cit.*

the labyrinthine web of the student terrorist groups. He had increasingly violent clashes with Masferrer and the co-leader of the MSR, Manolo Castro. On one occasion, Masferrer and Fidel Castro met without premeditation and exchanged fire from their cars. At another time, Castro and one of his goons ambushed Masferrer and tried to gun him down, but their intended victim returned fire and they retreated from the scene.

The rivalry between the revolutionary faction leaders appears to have been primarily personal. Unlike Fidel Castro, Masferrer came from a distinguished family which had played a prominent role in the struggle for Cuban independence. Where Castro was merely a student with a remarkable memory for detail and superlative gifts for conspiracy and insurrectionary leadership, Masferrer was one of the most brilliant men the University had ever graduated. He had won the coveted Dolz Prize and the title of Eminent Alumnus of the University. The fact that both men came from Oriente had not prevented Masferrer from characterizing Fidel Castro as an uncouth rural clown.

Whether there were also political aspects to the rivalry is a difficult question to answer. As a very young man, Rolando Masferrer had fought in the ranks of the Spanish Loyalist forces and had been wounded in the leg by a grenade. He was a militant member of the Communist Party at the time. Later he left the Party and eventually became strongly anti-Communist. In 1947 and 1948, both he and Manolo Castro were leftists, but their attitude toward the Communist Party is a subject of dispute.

After talking to several Cuban exiles who refused to be identified publicly because of fear of reprisals against their families, Martin and Santora came up with the following circumstantial story:

Fidel Castro boasted publicly that he was going to kill Manolo, his reason being jealousy of the latter's prestige among the University students. At a meeting of the UIR, Fidel Castro forced through a decision condemning his rival to death.[6]

At about 11 P.M. of February 22, 1948, Manolo Castro was standing outside the movie house, *Cinecito,* in downtown Havana, of which he was part owner, talking and joking with friends. Suddenly, the group was caught in a murderous burst of fire which killed Manolo Castro and a friend, wounded two other people, sent bystanders scurrying for shelter and shattered the plate glass windows in neighboring jewelry stores.

Fidel Castro and three other students were immediately picked up on suspicion of murder. A police officer had seen one of Castro's gang, a certain Gustavo Ortiz Faez, running near the scene of the crime. Ortiz Faez was arrested. Unfortunately, he turned out to be a nephew of President Grau San Martin, and political heat was turned on the police department and the judge handling the case.

The evidence of this heat is that Judge José-Maria Gispert, came to the Third Police Station, where Fidel and friends were being held, conducted an informal investigation and then dismissed the charges because of insufficient evidence. The reason given for bringing the magistrate to the prisoners rather than vice versa was "a rumor that armed men were going to assault the court and kill the students."[7] Presumably, this was a reference to Masferrer's MSR, of which Manolo Castro had been a director, but it was ridiculous to suppose that the Cuban police was unable to protect prisoners in a court of law.

El Mundo of February 26th characterized the murder of Manolo Castro as a link in a chain of "implacable terrorism," creating an "atmosphere of savage hatreds, wherein no means of elimination of an adversary is repudiated." Unless law and order were promptly restored, the editorial con-

---

[6] *op. cit.,* 7th article.
[7] *Havana Post,* February 27, 1948.

tinued, Cubans would "lose our status as a civilized people and fall into the category of primitive societies in which the indiscriminate will of the strongest is imposed."

While Fidel Castro had escaped being put on trial for the Manolo Castro killing, his position was becoming precarious. His political crony and patron in the police department, the homicidal Major Emilio Tró, had been killed in a wild gun battle five months before. Rival factions of terrorists within the police department had shot it out in the Havana suburb of Marianao, killing six people and wounding twelve, among the latter a baby.

It was less than two months after the Manolo Castro business that Fidel went to Bogotá and took part in the Communist-organized holocaust there in the manner already described.

When he returned to Havana, he found that Sergeant Oscar Fernandez Caral of the University police, who had been a friend of Manolo Castro, had promised to bring him to justice for the murder. On July 4, 1948, Caral was shot to death and, according to the police dossier, Fidel Castro was "identified" as an author of the crime. He was promptly arrested and summoned before Federal Judge José M. Gispert. Witnesses to the killing were apparently afraid of reprisals by the sinister murder organization with which Castro was associated and they refused to testify. Under these circumstances, the Prosecuting Attorney of the Court of Appeals was compelled to order Fidel Castro's release.

Havana was unsafe for the student gunman and he spent the rest of the summer and fall hiding out at Biran. In October, he married Mirtha Diaz Balart in a church guarded by soldiers loyal to the families of bride and groom. The young Castros spent their honeymoon in the United States beyond the reach either of rival terrorist organizations or of the feeble clutch of Cuban criminal law.

That is about all that can be ascertained at this time and at this distance concerning the strand of crime and terrorism in the youth and early manhood of Fidel Castro. The other and more important strand was Communism. Here again, the student years were formative and here again the trail has been overgrown by time and space and by the facilities always available to a dictatorship to destroy records and silence living witnesses.

6

Castro and the Communist Party

> "The real philosophers,
> however, are commanders
> and lawgivers; they say:
> 'Thus shall it be!'"
> —Friedrich Nietzsche
> Beyond Good and Evil

URING the youth and adolescence of Fidel Castro, the Communist Party floated on a high tide of power and influence. The Party had been organized in the 1920's by a group of intellectuals in Havana University. One of its charter members and early leaders was Raul Roa, whom Fidel Castro would later appoint Foreign Minister of Cuba.

The first General Secretary of the Cuban Communist Party was the brilliant Julio Antonio Mella, who was driven into Mexican exile by the Machado regime and murdered there in 1929.[1] Leadership of the Communist Party was soon assumed by Juan Marinello, a poet and literary critic of some note and a member of the planter plutocracy.

[1] The best account of this assassination is contained in Bertram D. Wolfe, *Diego Rivera*, Knopf, New York, 1939, pp. 254-7. Wolfe, a former leader of the American Communist Party, blames Machado's *Porra* for the death of Mella. More recently, Victor Alba has claimed that a Soviet double agent committed the murder, *Historia del comunismo en America latina*, Mexico, 1954. Ralph de Toledano, in his autobiographical *Lament for a Generation*, Farrar, Straus & Cudahy, New York, 1960, pins the crime on the well-known Comintern agent Vittorio Vidali, alias Carlos Contreras.

The Communists played an equivocal role in the overthrow of the Machado dictatorship, but flourished in the ensuing period of chaos and revolutionary ferment. In early 1934, they were able to call a congress of their controlled trade union movement with 10,000 delegates present and in the same year they started the foolhardy practice of setting up soviets in the sugar mills. The Communists tried to overthrow the weak, leftist regime of Grau San Martin by strikes and insurrectionary activity, but Batista stepped in, ousted Grau and used military force to restore some semblance of order.

In the late 1930's, the Communist Party espoused the world-wide popular front policy and, under Moscow orders, offered Batista its support. Protracted negotiations followed in which representatives of the Soviet Government met with Batista.[2] In 1938, the Cuban Communist Party was legalized for the first time in its history; the trade unions were reorganized shortly thereafter under Communist control and the Reds were given key posts in the Labor Department. In the July 1940 elections, the Communist Party gave all-out support to Batista. The Party elected ten members to the Chamber of Deputies and a Red mayor in Santiago, the second largest city in the Republic. In March 1943, Juan Marinello joined the Bastista government as Minister without Portfolio, thus becoming the first open Communist to enter a Western Hemisphere cabinet.

The honeymoon continued until 1947. The number of enrolled Communist voters rose from 90,000 in 1940 to 150,-000 in 1946.[3] In the first years of the Grau San Martin administration, the Communists attained dizzying heights of prestige and power. The Cuban President gave the Red-dominated Cuban Confederation of Labor $750,000 to build

[2] Information which the writer received verbally in 1939 from a Mexican diplomat who attended some of these meetings and who was a Soviet agent.
[3] Robert J. Alexander, *Communism in Latin America*, Rutgers University Press, New Brunswick, N. J., 1957, pp. 283-4.

a Workers' Palace. When the Red unions made unreasonable wage demands and went on strike, the Government would sometimes expropriate the recalcitrant enterprises.

On March 6, 1946, the Educational Association of Cuba sounded the alarm against rapidly spreading Communist influence in the schools and stated that the Reds had an iron grip on the teaching profession. Although the U.S.S.R. did very little business with Cuba, its Legation contained fifty staff members. Lavish entertainment and effective "cultural" propaganda were supplied by the Legation.[4] What was considerably more sinister was that Cuba was becoming one of the main Latin American centers of espionage and other apparatus activities.

The State Department Influence

In coddling Communism, the Batista and Grau regimes were following United States policies. During the latter part of the popular front era (1937-39) and the years of the war alliance (1941-45), Americans who denounced Communism or called the U.S.S.R. a totalitarian state risked being accused of giving aid and comfort to Nazi Germany. While there were no Communist cabinet members in the Roosevelt Administration, men of equal power in the U. S. Government were covert Soviet agents.

At the time that Batista was negotiating with the Cuban Communist Party, the State Department official in charge of Latin American affairs was Laurence Duggan. According to the sworn testimony of former Soviet courier Hede Massing, Duggan was recruited into an OGPU spy network in the 1930's.[5] With a Soviet agent in this strategic position, it was inevitable that strong pressures would be exerted to see that "reactionaries" were eliminated from Latin American

[4] Phillips, *op. cit.*, pp. 229, 232-3.
[5] Senate Internal Security Subcommittee, *Hearings on the Institute of Pacific Relations*, pp. 235-7.

posts in the American Foreign Service and replaced by leftists.

The full mystery of Duggan's role in United States policy toward Latin America will never be solved. In 1948, after extensive F.B.I. interrogation, he plunged or was pushed to his death from a window of his New York office.

The Cuban Communist Party managed to hold its own in 1939-41 when Hitler Germany and Stalinist Russia were bound by perfidious pacts of neutrality and friendship. The Cuban Reds at that time, like their confrères everywhere else in the world, were engaged in savage attacks on the United States and on the policy of aiding the democracies. The United States Government obviously did not approve of Communist influence in Latin America in that period, but influential figures in the U.S. political and labor movement were seemingly indifferent to it.

The Second Inter-American Labor Conference opened on December 1, 1939 at Havana. Vicente Lombardo Toledano, leader of the Communist-dominated Confederation of Latin American Labor and a top Soviet agent in the Western Hemisphere, declared that the Good Neighbor policy was dead, and called on the workers to back the "peace policies of the Soviet Union." Lazaro Peña, one of the leading Communists in the Cuban labor movement, joined in the diatribes against the United States.

"James B. Carey, secretary of the Congress of Industrial Organizations (CIO) of the United States, told a cheering group of workers in Havana that one of the principal aims of the CIO was to keep out of the European conflict. Neither he, nor Kathryn Lewis, daughter of John L. Lewis, who sat on the platform, listening to the attack on the United States, said one word in defense of their country." [6]

[6] Phillips, *op. cit.*, p. 195.

Red Links at the University

There is a difference of opinion as to precisely when Fidel Castro definitely espoused Communism. According to Dr. Emilio Nuñez Portuondo, who was a member of the general secretariat of the Cuban Senate at the time, Fidel Castro subordinated himself to Communist Party discipline during his first year at the University (1945-46) and used the Party name of Fidelio.

Castro's former brother-in-law, Rafael Diaz Balart, gives basically the same account. "Right when he started at the University in 1945," Balart testified, "it was very easy for him, and at the same time for the Communists that had and always have had a very powerful branch in the University of Havana—it was very easy for both of them to get to a very nice understanding . . ."[7]

Fidel Castro told Balart, when they were both University students, "that he was going to go with the Communists because it was the best way for a young leader who was thinking of the future to promote himself to the highest rank." The witness added that the Communists "needed a front man (at the University), and Fidel needed them to back him."

Diaz Balart was careful to add that "Castro is not a card holder of the Communist Party in Cuba, never has been . . . What happens is that Castro is a member of the Third International, which they don't have a card, never.

"I want to affirm, with all my faith and all my knowledge, that Fidel Castro is the most important and most dangerous [agent] in the Western Hemisphere of the Communist International machinery since the Russian Revolution."

Balart testified that, while he was at the University, Fidel

[7] Senate Internal Security Subcommittee, *Hearings*, May 3, 1960. I am unable to give page references because the quotations are from the typed transcript, the hearings being at this writing in the hands of the printer.

Castro had dealings with Leonel Soto and Alfredo Guevara. These men were the top Communist leaders on the campus and were directly responsible to the Political Bureau of the Party. After taking power, Fidel Castro made Alfredo Guevara director of the educational and indoctrination program of the Cuban armed forces.

He was also associated with Flavio Bravo, Valdes Viveo and Mas Martin, young Communist activists in the University of less importance than the other two. Balart testified that he was told at the time that Fidel Castro, while a student, had dealings with Fabio Grobart, the Polish-born agent who "had long been the leading light in the underground organization" [8] of Communist and Soviet activities in Cuba and who was expelled from the island by President Prio Socarrás for subversive activities.

Francisco Chao Hermida was at the University with Fidel Castro and in the UIR. On the latter's return from the Bogotazo, Chao noted that he associated closely with the Communist campus leaders, Soto and Guevara. At that point, Chao Hermida came to the conclusion that Fidel Castro had turned Communist.

According to Diaz Balart, Soto and Guevara realized that Fidel Castro was a natural leader of the masses. They concentrated on his indoctrination and plied him with Marxist-Leninist literature. Castro, it was said, was enormously impressed with *The Communist Manifesto*, the eloquent pamphlet published by Marx and Engels during the 1848 revolution. Fidel does not seem to have been either a deep or assiduous student of Marxism. His nature was too restless and his emotional needs too exigent.

From the standpoint of the Communist Party, it was essential that Fidel Castro sever his connections with the student murder gangs, both because he was destroying his potential future usefulness as a national leader and because the Party did not control these terrorist groups and naturally

[8] Alexander, *op. cit.*, 293.

preferred to have Fidel dependent exclusively upon it. Diaz Balart believes that Fidel Castro made an agreement along these lines with Guevara and Soto and that, in return, he was allowed to take a prominent role in student political movements which the Communists dominated. Castro took a leading position in a movement to force a lowering of bus fares and managed to get himself photographed among Cuban Communist and other leftwing leaders beside an overturned bus which his mob had set on fire.

"In the student demonstrations," write Emma and Lidia Castro, "Fidel was always in the forefront and once he was seriously wounded in the head in a violent encounter with the police. But he recovered and continued fighting without withdrawing because of this handicap." [9]

Whatever the exact terms of his agreement with Soto and Guevara may have been, it is significant that there is no testimony, no gossip or police dossier entries linking him with acts of individual terrorism after July 4, 1948, the date of the murder of Sergeant Caral. This does not mean that he abstained from killing individuals. On the contrary, his entire career would be punctuated by murders and illegal executions. But, after 1948, he seems to have given up individual terrorism of the anarchist variety, in which individuals were killed for personal or factional reasons without any relationship to a broad strategy for the conquest of power.

During his first years at the University, Fidel did practically no academic work and completed only a fraction of the courses needed for his diploma.

"Meanwhile, papa was so preoccupied because Fidel was making very little progress in his studies," Emma and Lidia Castro wrote. "And that was natural. He said: 'Politics will be his glory or ruin. How is it possible for him to spend his time making speeches and at the same time study? We are

[9] *op. cit.*, 2nd article. Unfriendly sources claim that the wound was of no importance, but that Fidel squeezed dramatic value out of the episode by wearing a large white bandage around his head.

wasting money and Fidel should return to Biran to work and give up this restless path which is so thorny with difficulties . . .' " [10]

Fidel Castro did work hard at his studies from the time of his marriage in 1948 to his graduation in 1950. He relied on a prodigious memory and powerful physique and could keep going on cognac and benzedrine.[11] Moreover, he could count on pro-Communist professors to see that he got passing grades.

In October 1950, Fidel Castro received his diploma as a Doctor of Laws. According to the Castro sisters, "Papa wanted to send him to the Sorbonne in Paris for two years and then to Oxford for two years so he could specialize in economics, which was his chosen field, and he had accepted the proposal in principle." [12]

This, however, was not to be. The pressing exigencies of Cuban politics made Castro decide to stay at home and plunge into the maelstrom.

In the Orthodox Party

Meanwhile, the winds that had been blowing so consistently in favor of Cuban Communism began to change direction. President Grau's support of Red leadership in the trade unions had undermined the once powerful labor movement of Grau's own party, the *Autenticos*. Moreover, the flagrant corruption, which Grau tolerated and from which he profited, had disgusted the majority of the revolutionary terrorist organizations which had been his strongest supporters.

In the spring of 1947, Senator Eduardo Chibas, a veteran supporter of President Grau, turned against him and launched a new political organization called the Cuban People's Party. The ABC organization promptly deserted Grau

[10] Emma and Lidia Castro, *op. cit.*, 2nd article.
[11] Martin and Santora, *op. cit.*, 7th article.
[12] *op. cit.*, 4th article.

for Chibas, and the Communist Party also moved into opposition to the Grau regime.

The Cuban People's Party called itself the Orthodox Party, the implication being that they were the only orthodox *Autenticos*, the rest having been led by Grau into the quagmires of corruption. The new party was a one-man show and a personal instrument of Eddie Chibas. The leader was a spell-binder richly endowed with charisma. His Sunday evening radio program, which had the highest audience rating in Cuba, was dedicated to the exposure of corruption in high places, citing names, dates, facts and figures. Eddie Chibas also sang what he called war chants and worked himself and his audience into emotional states reminiscent of hillbilly revival meetings.

It was said that one could walk down the residential district of any Cuban city on Sunday night without missing a sentence of Chibas' angry broadcasts. As the raucous, gravelly voice faded out, it would begin to come in strong from the next house down the road which had door and windows open to the tropical night and loudspeaker on full blast.

Chibas was also an ultra-nationalist and a man who knew how to play on the feelings of inferiority and resentment of the politically leftist Cuban masses. According to Batista's biographer, Edmund A. Chester, a hostile source, Chibas was "a fanatic who conveyed his fanaticism to the thousands who followed him blindly in any direction he chose to move . . . His enemies said he was insane and his friends said he was a defender of the underprivileged." [13]

The Communist Party tried to get on the bandwagon and began to denounce corruption in high places at about the same time as Chibas. Early in 1948, the Party published an open letter to President Grau in which it demanded the dismissal of Minister of Education José Aleman and another

[13] Edmund A. Chester, *A Sergeant Named Batista*, Henry Holt, New York, 1954, p. 220.

member of the Cabinet who was reputed to be equally crooked.

With his political machine threatened with disintegration, Grau turned on the Communists. In 1947, Eusebio Mujal, a former Communist, rallied the *Autentico* labor forces against Red domination, but was beaten in a trade union convention packed with paper unions. Mujal and the *Autenticos* walked out.

Meanwhile, Grau had appointed Dr. Carlos Prio Socarrás, the 42-year-old veteran leader of the student revolutionaries of the Machado era, Minister of Labor.[14] In mid-1947, Prio Socarrás had the Communist labor leaders ousted from the Workers' Palace on the grounds that the legitimate leaders of the trade union federation were the *Autenticos*. Later that year, Lazaro Peña and 125 other Communist Party activists were arrested. In 1948, the Grau government confiscated *Mil Diez*, one of the chief propaganda vehicles of Communism. Dr. Prio Socarrás was nominated as the *Autentico* candidate for President of Cuba and began his campaign in the summer of 1948.

"The first step is to remove the mask of the Communists and expose their ultimate aim of world domination," he declared. "My idea is to destroy the Communist Party in Cuba."[15]

The Communist Party prepared to go underground. In part, this was a reaction to growing repression, in the course of which some Communist labor leaders were gunned down. The broader political picture was that the cold war was gathering momentum and the United States was engaged in a swift and painful reassessment of the aims and character of international Communism.

The years of transition were 1947 and 1948. In the United States, these were the years of the Truman Doctrine, Eliza-

[14] Secretary General of the Student Directorate of Havana University in 1930; three years in a Machado prison; a founder of the *Autentico* Party, and one of the authors of the Cuban Constitution of 1940. v. Phillips, pp. 239-46.
[15] Phillips, p. 245.

beth Bentley's exposure of Soviet spies in the U. S. Government, the investigation of Alger Hiss by the House Committee on Un-American Activities, and the indictment of the top leaders of the American Communist Party for seditious conspiracy.

The American Communist Party made preparations for illegality and the Cuban Communist Party followed suit. It was logical to assume that gathering American opposition to Communism would have comparable repercussions in Cuba. This at least had been the pattern of the past.

This precarious political situation dictated that those members and sympathizers of the Cuban Communist Party who were not irrevocably branded with the Red label work inside other and more respectable organizations.

Fidel Castro joined the ranks of Eddie Chibas' Orthodox Party. According to the not-always-trustworthy testimony of his sisters, Fidel "embraced with all the enthusiasm of his fiery youth the ideals of this man [Chibas] who emerged as a reformer . . ." [16] Emma and Lidia suggest, without directly saying so, that Fidel Castro was a charter member of the Orthodox Party.

Despite Castro's energy and driving ambition, he was not able to get into the leadership of the new political machine. On several occasions, Eddie Chibas told his closest associates that Fidel Castro was a gangster and a man who should never be trusted.[17]

Chibas had aroused the anger of the Cuban people against persons elected to positions of trust who engaged in unconscionable thefts of public funds. By 1948, he was a voice in the land, by 1950 a major political power. It seemed clear that he would run for Presidency of Cuba in 1952 and probable that he would be elected.

In July 1951, Chibas promised his radio audience conclu-

[16] op. cit., 2nd article.
[17] Statement to the writer by Dr. Carlos Marquez Sterling, the 1958 candidate of the Orthodox Party for the Presidency of Cuba.

sive proof of graft by a member of Prio's Cabinet. Then the people who had promised to give him the documentary proof decided not to do so. On August 5, 1951, Chibas stepped before the microphone with his vast audience eagerly awaiting the promised proof of wrong-doing in high places and with the private knowledge that he could not comply with his pledge. Chibas gave a highly emotional speech, then pulled a pistol out of his pocket and shot himself fatally.

Friends attributed his suicide to despondency over being obliged to retract an accusation he knew to be true and despair at the apparent hopelessness of dragging the Cuban government from the morass of venality. Chibas had believed that he could best arouse the nation by killing himself during his broadcast. Ironically, he had gone over his time limit and, at the moment he fired his gun, was off the air.

After this tragedy, the powerful and rapidly growing Orthodox Party reorganized with Dr. Roberto Agramonte as standard bearer. Behind Agramonte was the ghost of Chibas; the deep waves of popular emotion stirred up by the latter's suicide made it seem a foregone conclusion that the Orthodox Party would elect its candidate President.[18]

Fidel Castro was elected to the municipal, provincial and national assemblies of the Orthodox Party, but these were large bodies with little influence on party policy. He was not named to the corresponding executive committees.[19] As a member of the Havana municipal assembly, Castro was subordinate to Dr. Carlos Marquez Sterling, an economics professor at Havana University and a powerful figure in the Orthodox Party. Sterling remembered a warning by Chibas that Castro was not to be trusted. He also considered that Fidel was anarchistic, undisciplined and apparently "communistic."[20]

[18] Phillips, p. 256; Alexander, p. 290.
[19] Statement of Dr. Carlos Marquez Sterling to the writer.
[20] *Idem.*

Nevertheless, Fidel Castro was nominated as one of the Orthodox candidates for the Chamber of Deputies from Havana. His political prospects looked bright. Nationally, the Orthodox Party was expected to take the elections with a comfortable majority, with the *Autenticos* in second place and the followers of Batista running a poor third. Meanwhile, in the process of moving toward illegality, the Communist Party had been energetically infiltrating its cadres—at least those which were not hopelessly compromised by open Party activity—into the Orthodox and *Autentico* groups, particularly the former.

In 1951, members of the Balart family, who supported Batista, arranged a secret meeting between the former Cuban strong man and Fidel Castro. The conference occurred at Batista's *finca*. It was amicable, but Castro nevertheless refused to give Batista political support in return for future favors. News of the meeting leaked out and was misinterpreted. The newspaper commentator, Mario Kuchilan, publicly denounced Fidel Castro for having sold out to Batista.

Then, in March 1952, Fidel Castro's immediate political prospects were suddenly shattered. Facing a possible defeat at the polls, Fulgencio Batista moved troops into key positions and seized power in a virtually bloodless coup d'etat. This was done on the weak pretext that he was forestalling a similar putsch by President Prio Socarrás. Batista called off the elections, dissolved Congress, banned strikes and suspended constitutional guarantees for a 45-day period. Cuban democracy had gone out with a whimper.

7

Moncada: The Dress Rehearsal

> "But was it the truth? Nowhere has truth so short a life as in Sicily; a fact has scarcely happened five minutes before its genuine kernel has vanished, been camouflaged, embellished, disfigured, squashed, annihilated by imagination and self-interest; shame, fear, generosity, malice, opportunism, charity, all the passions, good as well as evil, fling themselves onto the fact and tear it to pieces; very soon it has vanished altogether."
>
> —Giuseppe di Lampedusa
> *The Leopard*

Eleven days after the seizure of power by Batista in March 1952, two Soviet couriers arrived at the Havana airport from Mexico on diplomatic passports. A Cuban lieutenant decided that these men should be searched, together with their luggage, regardless of diplomatic immunity. The couriers, Fedor Zaikog and Alex Selatoz, refused to permit this and returned to Mexico. The Batista government backed the decision of the young lieutenant and on April 3rd the Soviet Union broke diplomatic relations with Cuba.

Swift repressive measures against the Communist Party of Cuba (or People's Socialist Party, as it called itself) followed, forcing it to go underground. The top party leaders, Blas Roca, Juan Marinello and Lazaro Peña, were jailed, then allowed to leave the island.

The Soviet Legation in Cuba, which had given diplomatic immunity to 200 officials and employees, many of whom were engaged in courier work, forging passports and financing other Latin American Communist Parties, was closed down and the building nationalized. The secret headquarters of the Cominform in Havana was shut down and five of its top agents were recalled to Russia. Within weeks of Batista's coup d'etat, the Soviets were obliged to shift the headquarters of their subversive apparata in the Caribbean from Cuba to Mexico.

In the light of the allegations that would later be made by propagandists serving the Fidel Castro rebellion that Castro fought Communism, whereas Batista covertly supported it, the contemporary reaction of informed observers to these events is of interest. Ruby Hart Phillips, the *New York Times* bureau chief in Havana, wrote a forceful article about Batista's vigorous suppression of Communism in Cuba.[1] The verdict of Anthony T. Bouscaren was: "For many years Cuba was considered to be the center of Soviet operations for Latin American Communism. The return to power of General Fulgencio Batista in early March 1952 changed all that, however." [2] Even Robert J. Alexander grudgingly conceded that "the (Communist) Party became

[1] April 6, 1952.
[2] *Imperial Communism*, Public Affairs Press, Washington, D. C., 1953, p. 217.

increasingly hostile to the (Batista) regime" and that "Batista himself soon moved against the P.S.P." [3]

Fidel Castro promptly reacted with bold defiance of the Batista dictatorship. On March 24th, less than a week after the seizure of the Soviet couriers, he submitted on his own initiative a brief to the Urgency Court which charged Batista with treason to the Cuban Constitution and demanded his condemnation. This act must have seemed impressive evidence of Castro's devotion to democracy to those Cubans who forgot, or never knew, that only four years previously Fidel Castro had fought to drown the democratically elected Conservative government of Colombia in a sea of blood.

The main opposition to Batista's seizure of power came from Cuban liberals who were devoted to democracy and wanted neither military nor Communist dictatorship. In 1953, leaders of the Orthodox and Authentic parties met in Montreal to forge a united front against Batista. Strong pressure developed within the Orthodox Party to transform the opposition movement into a Popular Front, in which the Communist Party would participate.

As Dale Francis described the sequence of events in *Our Sunday Visitor* for March 20, 1959: "Quite aside from the evil of Communism, this would have been disastrous, for it would have given Batista a chance to stamp his opposition as Red. There was never any serious consideration given by the ten party leaders to this proposal for a popular front and there was an anti-Communist resolution offered by the Authentic party.

"This resolution was strongly opposed by some of the Orthodox representatives because they feared the pressure group in their party. Finally the resolution was dropped from the public statement. All of this was not made public

[3] *op. cit.*, p. 293. We say "even Alexander" because the industrious and not untalented historian of Latin American Communism is a socialist, who preaches the naïve, and historically inaccurate, doctrine that the only effective way of combatting Communism is to install leftwing governments of an independent variety.

and there would be no purpose in making it public now except for the fact that the man back in Cuba who had pressured the Orthodox representatives most strongly to include the Communist Party in the popular front was Fidel Castro.

"When the Orthodox representatives returned, he blasted them because they had not done as he had told them. Their explanation that they had at least prevented the anti-Communist resolution was angrily dismissed by Castro. He said that, seeing how little influence he had in the Orthodox Party, he'd start his own movement. Soon after that there was the attack on the barracks at Santiago, and the 26th of July movement was born."

This information was revealed to Dale Francis by a man who has known Castro for years "and who has remained close to him since his arrival in Havana." It is entirely confirmed by Dr. Carlos Marquez Sterling, one of the chief Orthodox Party leaders.

There are two intriguing entries concerning Fidel Castro in his police dossier for the first year of the Batista dictatorship, 1952-53. On September 8, 1952, the chief of the C1 Group of the Cuban National Police personally "captured" the occupants of a 1950 Chevrolet bearing license plate 50-310. "These turned out to be Fidel Castro Ruz, Miguel Rodriguez Lazo and Abel Santamaria Cuadrado, all of whom were returned to their homes after the corresponding investigations had been carried out." The entry does not explain why these people were arrested. It is interesting because Abel Santamaria Cuadrado was a militant activist in the Communist Youth Brigades.

There is also an entry for May 22, 1953. On that date, "the head of Department A of Group C1 of the Department of Investigation submitted a report to the head of the Department, in which he states that the Holandesa tearoom, located between Neptuno and San Rafael Streets, was a center of plotting and that opposition elements congregated there after 9 P.M. These elements belonged to the Orthodox Party, their leaders being Fidel Castro Ruz, Pardo Llada[4] and Roberto Agramonte, who were planning to plant bombs and other explosives in buses, public parks and other important establishments, for the purpose of enlisting sympathizers and arousing the public conscience so that the people would follow them in their revolutionary projects." The police report goes on to state that the conspirators were financed by ex-President Carlos Prio Socarrás and his right-hand man, Aureliano Sanchez Arango. It adds that they planned to liquidate Millo Ochoa and other elements within the Orthodox Party. If true, this is again significant, since Millo Ochoa was probably the most anti-Communist of all the Orthodox Party leaders.

Thus, the legend that Fidel Castro outgrew his youthful pro-Communist affiliations and became a liberal political leader within the Orthodox Party turns out to be as false as the interpretation of his work for the Soviets in Bogotá as just a youthful escapade. Within the Orthodox Party, he was distrusted as a Communist or Communist sympathizer, as a terrorist and gangster. He was known there as the leader of a faction fighting for a popular front which would have brought the suppressed and discredited Communist Party into a coalition with decent, freedom-loving Cubans. His espousal of the Orthodox movement occurred at a time when the Communist Party of Cuba was concentrating on infiltration of such movements and his defiance of dictator Batista occurred only a few days after the latter took steps to smash the Cominform apparatus and the Red propaganda machine which operated from the sanctuary of the Soviet Legation.

[4] "Pardo Llada is neither worse nor better than other Communists," *Patria*, Miami, May 20, 1960, p. 4.

The Rise of Raul Castro

Around 1950, Fidel's younger brother, Raul, entered Havana University as a student. In temperament, appearance and physique, he was very different from Fidel. Rafael Diaz Balart recalled him as a sensitive, emotional and intelligent person. This was a minority opinion. Girlish and effeminate in appearance, Raul soon showed himself to be cold and implacable, a man ideally suited to the role of Kremlin agent which he would later play.

According to Cuban exiles who knew him before he became a guerrilla leader, Raul Castro habitually associated with a homosexual clique. When fighting in the Sierra Maestra and the Sierra Cristal, the Castro guerrilleros grew mustaches and luxuriant beards. Raul was either unable or unwilling to do this and instead let his hair grow long and wore it in a feminine bun. Immediately after the victory of the insurgent forces, Raul married one of the top Soviet-trained leaders of the struggle, Vilma Espin, whose *nom de guerre* had been Deborah. This marriage was publicized despite the fact that the Castro leaders, as a rule, pursue the Stalinist practice of keeping their sexual and family lives private. For instance, the Cuban public has been told virtually nothing about Ilda Gadea, the Peruvian wife of Alfredo "Ché" Guevara.

When he took power, Fidel Castro named Raul to the post of Commander in Chief of the Cuban Armed Forces. For more than a year after this appointment, Raul continued to wear his hair long. Gossip within Cuba was coupled with a campaign of derision at his feminine habits in the Cuban refugee press, particularly *Patria* in Miami. Finally, the bun was cut off and, in the spring of 1960, press photographs revealed that Raul was wearing his hair as men do.

Raul Castro aroused mixed emotions in the breasts of some American correspondents. This ambivalence was exemplified by a two-page-long account of his visit to Raul's headquarters in the Sierra Cristal in 1958 by Charles Shaw, news director of WCAU, a Philadelphia radio and TV station.[5] This article incidentally belongs in any good collection of journalistic aberrations since it is probably the most foolish piece of pro-Castro writing ever published in the United States. An example of Shaw's political perspicacity is his suggestion that the Castro movement might be "essentially a Protestant effort to seize power in a predominantly Catholic country." Mr. Shaw's account of his encounter with Raul Castro reads in part as follows:

"In the distance, I could see two persons with long hair— hair hanging a good six inches below their shirt collars and apparently smooth faces . . . It wasn't until I was quite close and saw the wisps of beard on the face of the one in the striped shirt that I picked him as Raul and the other as Deborah . . .

"Raul's face, in repose, was the face of a boy, almost the face of a young woman. But when he talked, his face became that of a young man . . . The girls just stared, and when Raul smiled at them, I expected them all to swoon. They smiled back in ecstasy . . ." Reporter Shaw added the fatuous comment that, even after his brief association with Raul Castro, "I could not think of him as one whom I would like to have as a close friend."

Raul and Communism

When Raul Castro arrived at the University, Fidel turned him over to Alfredo Guevara and Leonel Soto, the two top Red leaders on the campus, for indoctrination. Rafael Diaz Balart testified that Raul became a seasoned Communist "because Fidel Castro put him in contact with the intellectual machinery of the Communist Party, Raul being a very young

[5] *Philadelphia Sunday Bulletin*, August 3, 1958.

man, and they indoctrinated him." The testimony continued:

Q: Do you remember telling us that Fidel Castro gave his brother copies of Marx's works?

A: Yes. That was part of the indoctrination that I just told you.

Q: How do you know he did?

A: Because I was there and I knew both of them.

After that, Raul was sent to the Soviet-bloc area for much more intensive training. The Cuban National Police dossier on Raul states merely that he proceeded to "countries behind the Iron Curtain while attending an International Conference on the Rights of Youth as a delegate."

As early as January 14, 1959, two weeks after the Castro forces seized power, Constantine Brown wrote an article for the *Washington Evening Star* excoriating the State Department for having deliberately chosen to ignore authoritative intelligence reports concerning the Communist backgrounds of both Fidel and Raul Castro. This prescient article casts some light on Raul's peregrinations and is worth quoting:

"Similarly, we rushed to recognize the new Cuban regime created by Fidel Castro. Off the record explanations in Washington are that we did so because the Cuban rebels replaced the dastardly dictatorship of Batista.

"Fidel Castro used to have a well-established reputation as a strong Communist sympathizer who organized the 1948 Bogotá demonstrations against Gen. George C. Marshall. His brother Raul was described as an outright Communist who had studied in Moscow the MVD techniques of guerrilla warfare against the forces of the capitalist dictators. *This appeared to be the information available to the highest official quarters in Washington before Castro started his rebellion and before it seemed that he might succeed.*

"Now all of a sudden he has been declared by the State Department to be lily white. There was nothing really tangible to go by, it was said, to show that Fidel had a hand in the anti-American uprisings in Bogotá in 1948 or that Raul had done anything more than have a good time in the Soviet Union." [6]

The State Department may have believed that Raul was merely sowing wild oats behind the Iron Curtain, but few other informed sources were equally naïve. In a well-informed and comprehensive article, "What Lies at the End of the Yenan Way?", J. L. Gomez Tello analyzed the Soviet political offensive in Latin America in February 1958. He had this to say about Raul Castro:

"Behind [Fidel] Castro is a small but powerful clique of poorly-disguised outright Communists. His brother *Raul* is an active pro-Communist, if not card-carrying member, who has attended party congresses in the Western Hemisphere and behind the Iron Curtain. His top military leader is *Guevara Cerna*, known as "el Ché," a party member of many years standing in Argentina, Guatemala and Mexico." [7]

U. S. News & World Report for April 20, 1959 quoted "a confidential intelligence memorandum on Fidel Castro and the people around him . . . by a 'non-U.S. agency.' This characterized Raul as "a dedicated Communist and the most dangerous of them all . . . He was married recently to Vilma Espin . . . She is a Communist and is known as a first-class hater. Raul is also violently anti-U.S."

The *Miami News* for April 26, 1959 reported: "Raul Castro—In the Communist category . . . Belonged to a Communist front group in University of Havana, received Red indoctrination in Prague and later joined Communist Youth Movement in Havana . . . His wife, Vilma, listed as a Communist Party member."

For obvious reasons, it is not possible to trace Raul's movements in the Soviet area with precision. According to a report by a Cuban refugee who cannot be identified, but who has outstanding intelligence sources at his disposal, Raul Cas-

[6] My emphasis—N.W.
[7] *Arriba,* Madrid, February 1958.

tro was instructed in sabotage and terrorism at the Soviet "Anticol" (Anti-Colonialism) school for international cadres at Melnik, a town about 25 miles north of Prague. The same source states that Raul proceeded to Moscow where he had an interview with Boris Ponomarev, a leading member of the foreign division of the Central Committee of the Soviet Communist Party (CPSU) and an inveterate manipulator of "Youth Festivals." This unidentifiable source has information, which he evaluates as unconfirmed, to the effect that Raul Castro was sent from the U.S.S.R. to Red China where he fought briefly in Chinese Red Army ranks against United States forces so that he would have practical training in military operations.

Prague was at the time the main center for the training of Communist militants from Asia, Africa and Latin America in sabotage, subversion and propaganda. According to documents of the Council Against Communist Aggression (headquarters Philadelphia and Washington, D. C.), there are at least three large independent training centers in Czechoslovakia. The so-called Institute of International Relations in the Zizkov district of Prague teaches 3,000 Czechs and 2,000 foreigners. This is the organization which caters primarily to Latin Americans. The Council reports:

"Although tuition at these centers mainly revolves around sabotage in all its forms, the main object of these academies is to turn out men capable of exercising influence over intellectual as well as labor circles in their own countries."

Until the end of Allied occupation of Austria in 1955, it was easy for foreign Communists to get into Czechoslovakia. All they had to do was go to Vienna, where the Russians would take them across the Soviet-patrolled Austro-Czech border.

Raul Castro returned from the Iron Curtain countries via Guatemala, which was then suffering under the Communist-dominated regime of Jacobo Arbenz. It was in Guatemala that Raul met Ernesto "Ché" Guevara, who would turn out to be the outstanding military leader of Fidel Castro's guerrilla operations.

Raul arrived in Havana on June 7, 1953 in the company of two Guatemalans, Bernardo Lemus Mendoza and Ricardo Ramirez Leon. The police found in Raul's possession "a large amount of Communist propaganda, including books in various languages, pamphlets, lectures, flags, banners, badges, all of a definitely Communist character and acquired behind the Iron Curtain while attending an International Conference on the Rights of Youth as a delegate. The other items seized consisted of phonograph records, motion picture films and pictures of the chief Russian leaders. A notebook was taken from the Guatemalan, RICARDO RAMIREZ, written in ink as a diary, which detailed interviews, dates and indicated with whom the interviews had been held by code numbers. It happens that, on their return from this trip, when they reached Panama, some of the Communist propaganda they carried was found after a search and confiscated.

"RAUL MODESTO CASTRO RUZ, apart from the Communist propaganda that was taken from him, was found to have in an inside pocket of his coat an article of four typewritten pages entitled 'Education in Cuba,' signed by him, and which was delivered at the Conference mentioned above. The article attacks various Cuban educational centers and political and labor organizations.

"As an additional detail of interest, it can be pointed out that the report stated that the two Guatemalans tried to leave Havana customs with their luggage even though they had said they were in transit. Since they had made no declaration, search was made, the result being to find the Communist propaganda already mentioned and with respect to which the President of the Havana Summary Court was immediately advised. He ordered the persons involved to be held at his disposition in the municipal guardroom." [8]

To be arrested as a Communist under Batista was a very

[8] Dossier of the Cuban National Police on Raul Castro.

serious matter indeed, but Raul Castro had influence. Fidel's brother-in-law, Rafael Lincoln Diaz Balart, was the former leader of the Batista youth movement and was by now Undersecretary of the Interior.

Testifying seven years later before the Senate Internal Security Subcommittee, Diaz Balart told how Raul Castro was caught by the police with Communist propaganda in his possession on his return from Prague and how Raul "talked with my brother, Waldo, and he told him that he was in prison but that he was ready not only to be in prison, but to die for the Communist cause."

The 26th of July

Having failed to inveigle itself into the united opposition of the liberal parties to the Batista dictatorship, the Cuban Communist apparatus decided to seize the initiative by a dramatic act of violence designed to shake Cuba out of its political sloth.

The original plan was to assassinate Batista.

A meeting of Communist Party leaders and University faculty and students hostile to the dictatorship was held in the University. Nine people attended, among them Blas Roca (real name, Francisco Calderio), the General Secretary of the Communist Party (PPS); the two student Red leaders, Leonel Soto and Alfredo Guevara; Raul Roa[9] and Antonio Nuñez Jiménez.[10] A seasoned fighter with practical experience in assassination and other acts of terror was needed to command the task force. Fidel Castro was chosen for the post.[11]

Fidel Castro started to train young activists at the Capel-

[9] Appointed Cuban Foreign Minister by the Castro regime.
[10] Named Director of the all-powerful Institute for National Agrarian Reform (INRI) by the Castro government.
[11] The source is the BRAC report, *Origin and Establishment of the Communist Party in Cuba*. This is basic for the background of the Moncada Barracks assault.

lania ranch in Pinar del Rio, a province to the west of Havana. While training was in progress, a golden opportunity presented itself. The Veterans of the Cuban War for Independence invited General Batista to attend a patriotic ceremony in Santiago de Cuba on July 13, 1953. This invitation and Batista's acceptance of it were carried in all Cuban newspapers.

Fidel Castro sent 50 men to Santiago. License plates and insignia were made to be placed on the cars of the assault force so they would seem to be vehicles of the Cuban Army. For the same reason, Cuban Army uniforms were obtained. The plan was to switch from the legal license plates to the falsified ones at the last moment, so that the attacking force would seem to be part of the police and military guard, its vehicles official and its openly displayed arms means of protecting the life of the dictator.

According to the BRAC report, this brilliantly conceived plan "would not have failed," except for the fact that the Cuban intelligence services got wind of it and persuaded Batista to cancel his trip to Santiago on one subterfuge or another.

Fidel Castro, who was in Havana, was summoned to appear before the Department of Investigations, but denied any knowledge of the conspiracy and was released. The assault group was still in Havana.

Meanwhile, the Communist leadership was considering a new and much more daring plan—the attack on the Moncada Barracks in Santiago. This barracks was garrisoned by the First "Maceo" Regiment, an infantry force of about a thousand men armed with modern weapons. In Santiago, two Castro agents, young Pedro Miret Prieto and the Communist, Aldo Santamaria Cuadrado, were ordered to make an intelligence reconnaissance of the garrison forces, their dispositions and the key points which should be seized in the event of an armed uprising. The local carnival was in full swing in Santiago. Therefore, it was easy for Miret and Santamaria to join military personnel in several nights of drinking and wenching. They reported the locations of the main caches for arms and ammunition to the Communist Party leaders in Havana, but pointed out that the proposed operation would be impossible without major reinforcement of the attack force.

A meeting was held in Havana on July 24th with Fidel Castro. The BRAC report quotes the Communist Party leader, Blas Roca, as stating at that gathering:

"Look here, today is Friday, the 24th, tomorrow is Saturday, the 25th, but, according to the report of the investigators, Miret and Santamaria, the most appropriate day is Sunday, the 26th. Almost all the officers will be away, since they are free Saturday night and go out to have fun. The enlisted men do the same. We will have to deal only with the guard which changes at 10:30 A.M. Well, we could get started at 5:30 A.M.; everything will be easy, and besides it is my name day." [12]

The attack force was built up to well over 100 activists. Some were supporters of ex-President Prio Socarrás, others were Communists or Caribbean Legion veterans; some University students joined and there was a smattering of Communists from Guatemala, the Dominican Republic and Venezuela.

Reporters Martin and Santora interviewed one of the survivors of the Moncada fiasco. He stated that they had ostensibly been recruited for a "shooting practice" session in the Oriente and had no inkling until the last moment that they would be committed to combat. "We arrived at a farm, the Finca Siboney, about three miles outside Santiago," this man recalled. "We were somewhat surprised to find guards posted at the doors to the houses and some of the men asked what in hell was going on." (The answer, which Fidel did not give, but might have, was that it is standard Com-

---

[12] The use of direct quotes suggests that the police had an agent or recording device in the room where the meeting took place.

munist operating procedure to throw an armed security cordon around any area where cadres are being trained, are meeting or are being readied for military action, the purpose of the cordon being to preserve secrecy by preventing spies from getting in or deserters and talkative elements from getting out.)

"It wasn't until dawn," the survivor reported, "that Fidel gave us an inkling of what we were to do. He told us then that we were going to take Moncada, that the members of the garrison were waiting to join us—a lie." [13]

They were issued a few pistols and .22 rifles half an hour before the attack was scheduled. Some of the men didn't know how to fire them.

The assault force moved toward the barracks in the pre-dawn hours of Sunday, July 26th, in a caravan of about two dozen cars. Some of the assault elements piled out of their cars and got lost. The survivor quoted by Martin and Santora estimated that only about 80 people took part in the actual operation.

All of the men, except for the physician, Dr. Muñoz, wore Cuban Army uniforms. In addition, there were two girls who were to serve as nurses. According to Fidel Castro's subsequent testimony at his trial, the invading force had no hand grenades, only one machine gun, "ten thousand cartridges of all calibers, and different types of weapons." [14] In his propagandistic and generally unreliable book on the Castro revolution, Ray Brennan claims that their only effective combat weapons "were three United States Army rifles, a half dozen Winchester rifles of Buffalo Bill vintage, and one machine gun with parts so worn out that it invariably developed stoppages after firing a burst or two." [15] (In this passage, reporter Brennan goes all out to make Castro and his men heroic underdogs. Fidel himself testified to having

[13] Martin and Santora, *op. cit.*, 2nd article.
[14] Jules Dubois, *op. cit.*, p. 43.
[15] Brennan, *op. cit.*, p. 18.

"three (not six) Winchesters of the time of Buffalo Bill;" the survivor mentions pistols and .22's. Nor is it credible that anybody planning a combat operation, designed to rely on surprise, would acquire 10,000 rounds for nine rifles.)

Regardless of what the actual equipment of the assailants was, clearly it was insufficient to achieve its purpose. The Moncada Barracks was occupied at the time by a skeleton force of able-bodied soldiers and by the sick troops in the infirmary. The soldiers at their posts were equipped with machine guns and modern infantry arms; hence, they not only occupied strong defensive positions, but had far superior fire-power. Moreover, it was predictable that the moment the carousing troops in the city heard the sound of gun fire, they would converge on the Moncada. This in fact happened.

Later, at his trial, Fidel Castro would answer that the insurrectionaries had counted on winning the garrison over to their side, then taking over the city of Santiago.

This explanation does not sound plausible. In 1953, there was practically no opposition to the Batista regime in Santiago de Cuba except among students and intellectuals. There was no reason on earth to assume that regular army forces would defect or that they would follow Fidel Castro, a student politician completely unknown to them. As the brilliant columnist for *El Mundo,* Jorge A. Horstmann, put it: "In Santiago de Cuba, there is no environment for politics. Nor for an insurrection. Nobody believes in anything. It is a desert without an oasis." [16]

An alternate explanation of the Moncada attack is that Castro and the Communist leadership wanted to make martyrs and create conditions in which the troops and police would retaliate against the attackers with a savagery and sadism that would shock the nation. On this point, the survivor of the adventure quoted by Martin and Santora stated:

[16] Jorge A. Horstmann, *Aguacero: 1074 'Goticas' Comentados,* Havana, 1956, No. 709.

"There is no doubt in my mind now that Castro knew the attack could not possibly succeed—but we didn't realize it then. We couldn't have known then that Castro was using us as pawns to build his reputation."

The most despicable crime charged against Fidel Castro and his followers in the Moncada attack is the murder of unarmed, bedridden soldiers in the infirmary. This accusation was made at the trial of Fidel Castro and his followers by Colonel Alberto del Rio Chaviano, who commanded the First Maceo Regiment, garrisoning the Moncada. "The report to the court," writes Dubois, "accused the rebels of having fired at will inside the hospital against occupants there, of having knifed three patients in the stomach, of having used dum-dum bullets and of having hurled hand grenades in the attack on Moncada." [17]

Fidel Castro "repudiated del Rio Chaviano's charge that knives had been used by the rebels in the Civil Hospital or anywhere else. He underscored the fact that none of his men was acquainted with the Military Hospital where they were charged with having killed soldiers." [18]

Fidel Castro's police dossier calls him "intellectual author and leader in the assault on the 'Moncada' Barracks where several members of the armed forces lost their lives, together with others who were assassinated while lying in the infirmary of the said barracks." The dossier on Raul contains an identical entry. The BRAC report states: "This is how the killing of the soldiers came about: on July 26th, at the Military Hospital, which was near the regimental headquarters, all the sick patients were stabbed to death; only one Chief saved his life. He had come in during the night, his gun had not been taken away and he had hidden it under his pillow."

Fidel Castro's denial of the charge of murdering defense-

[17] Dubois, *op. cit.*, p. 40.
[18] *Ibid*, pp. 44-5.

less invalids is singularly unconvincing. The statement that his force was not acquainted with the Military Hospital is dubious in view of the prior intelligence activity of his agents, Miret and Santamaria. Still less convincing is his denial that any of his men used knives. He had an assault force of from 80 to 120 men. The men without firearms obviously would not be sent into action without any weapons. They would not use clubs or bayonets because of the factor of surprise. Therefore, the obvious answer was knives or grenades.

The killing of these invalids enraged the rest of the soldiers and aroused their sadistic tendencies. The trapped insurgents surrendered after having been promised that their lives would be spared. According to pro-Castro sources, dozens of them were murdered and some tortured, blinded or castrated before being killed.[19] At his trial, Fidel Castro expatiated on these outrages; said that Moncada had been changed into a place of death and torture and added that "the walls were splattered with parts and particles of human bodies: skin, brains, human hair—not the marks of honorable death, but of bullets fired only a few inches from human bodies." [20] Judge Manuel Urrutia, later to be President of Cuba under Fidel Castro and still later to be ignominiously deposed because of his anti-Communist position, described the killings as "savage and barbaric" [21] and vainly asked President Batista to punish the guilty troops.

Thus, martyrs had been made; shocking crimes had been provoked; Fidel Castro had been given national stature, and thousands of decent Cubans had been shocked out of their complacent acceptance of dictatorship. All this had been achieved at practically no cost to the Communist apparatus. The main leaders of the Party had gone to Santiago, but stayed safely in the background.

19 Brennan, *op. cit.*, pp. 22-25.
20 Phillips, *op. cit.*, p. 268.
21 Brennan, *op. cit.*, p. 25.

Neither Fidel nor Raul invaded hospital or barracks, the two death traps of the 26th of July. Raul was sent with a detachment of 22 men to seize the Palace of Justice and set up a machine gun there. The Palace was deserted in the early hours of the morning and Raul was able to accomplish his mission without incident, getting away when it was clear that the attempt had fizzled.

The whereabouts of Fidel Castro during the fighting is something of a mystery. Brennan's story is that the lead car of the motorcade got through the barracks gate without incident, but that when the second car, with Fidel Castro in it, attempted to pass, the alarm bell sounded. Thereupon, Fidel "made the mistake that may have cost the battle. He stopped the car, which he was driving, long enough to take the sentry prisoner." [22] After that, Brennan says, the fire was so intense that Fidel Castro ordered a general withdrawal. If one concentrates on the statements of fact Brennan makes and ignores his conjectures as to motivation, there is a clear implication of callousness or cowardice. Fidel Castro allowed the lead car to get into the barracks. Then, seeing that there would be counterfire, he abandoned his car, thus blocking the motorcade behind him and condemning the trapped lead elements to defeat and death.

The survivor of the slaughter who talked to reporters Martin and Santora gives an account which is close in factual sequence to, though very different in interpretation of motive from, the Brennan version.

" 'The soldiers weren't surprised; we were,' said our informant wryly. 'They began chopping us down systematically. When Fidel saw the attack was failing, he said: "Every man for himself" and ran.

" 'Boris Santa Coloma was Haidee's sweetheart. He yelled, "What about the girls?" Castro yelled back, "We haven't time for that. I've given orders. We can't risk our lives."

---

[22] Brennan, op. cit., p. 18.

" 'Santa Coloma covered Castro while he fled. Then he went back to rescue the girls. He was shot to death.' " [23]

Jules Dubois tells an entirely different story. Fidel Castro decides to go to the most dangerous place, the fort (p. 33); he attacks what he believes is an arsenal, but it turns out to be a barbershop (p. 36); he hears heavy fire and orders a retreat (p. 36).

These three accounts agree on only two points. Fidel Castro did not penetrate either the fort or the hospital, the two areas of combat; that is quite obvious, because, if he had been in either place, he would have been killed. In the second place, he ordered a retreat when he heard answering fire. The accounts of Brennan and the two *Daily News* reporters agree on a third and more important matter: By ordering a retreat, Castro deserted his vanguard element, leaving it surrounded by the enemy and hence doomed.

Some Communists plunged into the death trap, notably Abel Santamaria, Castro's second in command.[24] The broad picture, however, was that the most important Communist cadres were spared. The liberals and the politically innocent were used as martyrs.

When the gunfire and the reprisals were over, four top leaders of Cuban Communism—Blas Roca, Joaquin Ordoqui, Bernardo Hernandez and Lazaro Peña—were arrested and indicted as accomplices and co-conspirators in the attempted insurrection. The four admitted that they had been in Santiago de Cuba at the time, but claimed that they had gone there solely to celebrate the name day of their leader, Blas Roca. At the trial, Fidel Castro was asked whether any lead-

[23] Martin and Santora, *op. cit.*, second article. It is worth noting that the eyewitness has Santa Coloma shot; Brennan, who was not there, has him sadistically castrated (*op. cit.*, p. 22.). There seem to have been savage reprisals, but most of the specific testimony on this point comes from Castro people, whose veracity is dubious in the extreme.

[24] At his trial, Fidel Castro was asked whether or not a book by Lenin was found on Santamaria's corpse. "It is possible," he replied, adding, "Anyone who was never interested in socialist literature is an ignoramus." Dubois, pp. 45-6.

ers of the Communist Party had been involved in the attempt. Castro denied that this was the case.

Thus, the shrewdness of Blas Roca in scheduling the attack for his name day paid off. There were few people in Cuba so naïve as to suppose that leaders of the Communist Party are in the habit of leaving the capital and traveling several hundred miles merely to celebrate the birthday or saint's day of the general secretary of the Party. But suspicion is not evidence. The judge, Manuel Urrutia, was a liberal who followed the evidence. Hence, the case against the four Party leaders was dismissed.

The 26th of July gave Castro the young martyrs and the blood legend he needed for a national movement. It had one other major effect. It hardened Batista against influential advisors who urged him to restore civil liberties and constitutional rights.

There may have been a chance of this in 1952 and early 1953. After Moncada, Batista reacted by pouring troops into Santiago, making wholesale arrests on suspicion and refusing to restrain ruthless military and police leaders who thought that the only way to deal with Communism was with brute force and blind terror.

A period of tightened dictatorship and intermittent civil war followed. All this enabled Fidel Castro to enlist honest men of good will to fight against the despotic situation which he had helped provoke.

At the time, Cuba had no death penalty. This was not an unmixed blessing, since it encouraged the soldiers and police to murder prisoners, alleging that they had attempted to escape, or else to kill them before they were officially taken into custody.

Orders had gone out that Fidel Castro was not to be taken alive. He was hidden and protected by Dr. Felipe Salcines, Rector of Santiago University. Dr. Salcines got the local organizations of the Lions and Rotary to intervene to save Fidel's life. It was Salcines who arranged to have the Archbishop of Mexico accept Castro's surrender and make a plea for an end of bloodshed.

Castro was tried by a civil court. Dr. Salcines and other Santiago professors helped Judge Urrutia write the verdict of the court, which imposed the comparatively mild penalties of 15 years imprisonment on Fidel and 13 years on Raul. Less than six years later, Castro became master of Cuba and revealed his lack of either gratitude or human decency by having Salcines dismissed from the University.

8

The Soviet Apparatuses

> "Sink into the mud, em-
> brace the butcher, but
> change the world. It needs
> it."
>
> —Bertholdt Brecht
> *Die Massnahme*[1]

I<small>N</small> PRISON, Fidel Castro became the leader of a group of tough trouble-makers and spent his spare time indoctrinating fellow convicts in Communism. A man who was in prison with him reported:

"Since he was somewhat of a scholar, he started giving history lessons to the less educated among the prisoners. When he was refused books on Marx, Engels and Lenin, he threatened a hunger strike. They gave him the books and he used them as texts, along with books on Cuban history. I know Cuban history and he distorted statements by Martí and others.

"When a priest and nuns came to the prison to conduct catechism classes, Fidel rejected the idea. He jeered at the men who accepted religious medals." [2]

The Diaz Balart family used its influence to get the Castro brothers amnestied; Mirtha pleaded with key newspaper edi-

---

[1] Translated by Arthur Koestler.
[2] Martin and Santora, *op. cit.*, 2nd article.

tors and radio program directors to advocate freedom for her husband. Batista, who would later be depicted in the United States as a monster of sadism and bloodthirsty vengeance, freed Fidel and Raul after they had served merely 22 months of their sentences.

When he returned to Havana, Castro found that his marriage was approaching shipwreck. Forced to choose between the Communist politics of her husband and the strongly pro-Batista position of her family, Mirtha decided in favor of family and separation was in time followed by divorce.[3]

In Havana, Fidel Castro openly announced his intention of overthrowing the Batista regime. In retaliation, the lackadaisical dictator neither imprisoned nor shot him. He merely banned him from the air waves—a procedure which Jules Dubois in his extraordinary book, characterizes as "obvious persecution." [4] What is obvious to this writer is that if an American launched armed insurrection against his government, he would not get off with 22 months in prison nor would he be given radio time, after his release, so that he could agitate for a second attempt at treason.

In July 1955, Castro departed for Mexico after first proclaiming that he would organize invasion of Cuba from that country. In Mexico City, he joined Raul, who had preceded him there and made advance arrangements.

In Mexico, Fidel Castro established contact with the key Soviet apparatuses operating in the Caribbean area. Since these organizations form a vital part of the story of Cuba and Communism, I shall make an effort to explain what they were and how they functioned. Unfortunately, it is very hard to do this. Since they are conspiratorial groups, only fragmentary data reach us, generally from counterintelligence agencies or from defectors. Moreover, they continu-

---

[3] A contributing factor in the divorce might have been two letters, one to his wife and a second to his mistress, written while he was in jail. Somehow they were inserted in the wrong envelopes.

[4] op. cit., p. 96.

ally change their names and functions, adding to the general confusion.

Latin American subversion was formerly under the control of the Sixth Section of the Foreign Secretariat of the Communist Party of the Soviet Union (CPSU). In recent years, this function has been transferred to two command organizations: OPU-YE (*Operatsionnoie Upravlenye*—Executive Bureau) in charge of general strategy and GUJA (*Glavnoye Upravlenye Iuzhnoi Ameriki*—Central Administration for South America), an executive organization concerned with the achievement of specific power goals which "has strongly de-emphasized the importance of political associations and ideology" and "seeks to carry Communism to power on the backs of non-Communist collaborators."

In addition, there is the *Junta de Liberación Latinoamericana*, Supreme Council of Latin American Liberation, consisting chiefly of Europeans—Russians, Germans, Hungarians, Czechs, Bulgarians and Spaniards—and engaged in training the future leaders of Latin American "liberation." Under the Junta, there is a special organization known as CESTA, which was organized in Guatemala in the spring of 1954 for terrorist activity. [5]

Early in 1956, "CESTA began an intensive training program both of its own personnel and those of allied or 'autonomous' affiliates.

"The impact of this training is still being felt—exploding bombs, Molotov cocktails, skilled assassinations—throughout the Caribbean.

"A Guatemalan 'Special Services' intelligence unit has compiled an enormous amount of data on this period—information still in the now-dusty files of the since-demoralized service in Guatemala City. Information includes a documentary report on the assassination of CESTA's first famous vic-

[5] To add to the complexity of the labyrinthine pattern of Soviet subversive apparatuses, each group has a code name which, of course, conceals its true nature and function. The code name of the Supreme Council of Latin American Liberation is CIUDAD.

tim: Nicaragua's President Anastasio Somoza, in October 1956." [6]

During most of the postwar period, Mexico has been the main operating center (as distinct from the higher command centers of Moscow and Prague) of Soviet subversion in Latin America. This includes espionage, terrorism, propaganda and political infiltration. The basic networks were created by Soviet Ambassador to Mexico Constantine Oumansky, a former high official of the OGPU. Oumansky was killed in an airplane crash in 1943, but his organization survived.

The exceptions to the rule of Mexican leadership have been Guatemala and Cuba. Under the pro-Communist regimes of Arévalo and Arbenz, various Soviet agencies were created in Guatemala which drew top personnel from apparatuses which had been operating in Mexico. Cuba became a center of intensive Soviet espionage penetration under Batista largely because of its great advantages as a Latin American communications center.

A detailed and comprehensive account of the relationship between the Soviet apparatuses in Mexico, Central America and the Caribbean and the Castro movement was published in the authoritative Chilean quarterly, *Estudios sobre el Comunismo* (Studies of Communism) in 1959 and 1960. The author, who uses the pseudonym of Pedro V. Domingo, is a journalist who covered the Spanish Civil War from both the Nationalist and the Loyalist sides, who then proceeded to Latin America, made an intensive study of Communism and Soviet penetration in that area and served as an adviser on these matters to a Latin American government. Domingo believes that Soviet subversion inevitably thrives under dictatorships.

In the fall of 1952, Francisco Martin, chief of the All-

[6] The organization and functioning of the Soviet apparatuses in Latin America is a subject on which *Carib* is excellently informed and its reports are factual and devoid of sensationalism. This is scarcely surprising in view of the fact that the Trujillo dicatorship has been a primary target of these apparatuses. These quotations are from that periodical.

Union Bureau for Aid to the Latin American Democracies (a dependency of GUJA—the Central Administration for South America) told the XIX Congress of the Secretariat for Foreign Affairs of the Central Committee of the Communist Party of the Soviet Union (CPSU) that the Communist Parties in Cuba and Guatemala had not carried out Moscow instructions. Specifically, ". . . the comrades responsible for the direction of the Party in that sector received very clear instructions four times during the last three months, ordering them to impose a *complete* abstention from every kind of activity, public or secret, which could be considered by the enemies of the working masses as tending toward the abolition of existing powers and governments." [7] What this meant was that the Communist Parties were to remain in the background and virtually dormant as opposition forces. In Guatemala, the reason for this was that Moscow feared that any revelation of the strength of the Communist Party inside the leftist government would alarm the United States and provoke successful counterrevolution or military intervention.

When the Guatemalan Communists persisted in their foolhardy course, the armed invasion that Moscow had predicted occurred and, in the summer of 1954, Colonel Castillo Armas ousted the Red regime. Several months before, according to Domingo, more than 85% of the personnel in the regional office of the AGENCIA CARIBE, a major Soviet apparatus for the Caribbean, had been shifted to Cuba.[8]

In Cuba, RAMBLA, another Soviet spy center for the Caribbean, was already scoring brilliant results under the direction of Roberto Palmero, an exceedingly competent Soviet agent who used a directorship of a large Havana transportation agency as his cover. A great deal of money was spent bribing Cuban personnel in the security agencies, the

[7] Pedro V. Domingo, "El Comunismo en el Caribe," *Estudios sobre el Comunismo*, Vols. VII & VIII, No's. 26 & 27 (Oct./Dec. 1959, pp. 93-99 and Jan./Mar. 1960, pp. 82-88, Santiago, Chile.

[8] *Ibid.* No page references because I am quoting from a translation of Domingo's article made by a U. S. Government agency.

Foreign Service and the Customs. Branch offices were set up in Varadero, Matanzas and Santiago.

By 1957, other Soviet apparatuses had been set up in Cuba, among them BANCO DEL SUR (Bank of the South), MEDICO (Physician), ORFEON, DESPACHO NORTE (Northern Office) and EL RODEO.

"In the agencies referred to above," Domingo writes, "the Cuban Communists, moreover, are few in number. They do not hold posts of leadership and they are used above all as 'guides,' but only if *nobody* in the circle in which they operate knows that they are members of the Communist Party. Almost all of them were recruited from the ranks of university youth and among the employees of trade unions."

By early 1958, almost a year before Batista's fall from power, these Soviet agencies had established contact with or penetrated the circles closest to Colonel Pérez Coujil, Chief of the Military Intelligence Service; General Pilar Garcia, Supreme Chief of the Cuban Police; General Hernando Hernandez, Chief of the Joint Staff of the Armed Forces; General Carlos Manuel Castillo, military commander of Matanzas and General Dámaso Sogo, military commander of Holguín.[9]

The Soviet agents were able to achieve these results for a variety of reasons. Roberto Palmero, the director of RAMBLA, often stayed at the millionaires' hotel, Dos Mares, at Varadero Beach. He associated with the rich, the well-informed and the powerful. Moreover, he was accepted by them. Palmero and his agents paid lavishly for the information they needed and for disloyalty. They were able to impress the Cuban counterintelligence agencies by giving them accurate and valuable information about the Cuban Communist Party, the leaders of which had already gone into hiding and the membership of which was divided and demoralized.

The Communist Party and its personnel were cynically sacrificed in order to consolidate the position of the Soviet apparatuses with the Batista security organizations.

[9] *Ibid.*

All this intelligence information would be placed at the disposal of Fidel Castro's 26th of July Movement. As Domingo points out:

"These days everybody knows that the majority of the most outstanding successes of the 'liberating movement' of Castro were due to a careful reconnaissance of his adversary. Actually, so precise and complete a reconnaissance had not previously occurred in Latin America, not even in the course of the subversive activities of Colonel Juan Perón, although he had received adequate training in Europe."

The other vital link between Fidel Castro and the Soviet networks was an apparatus called A.T. (ASISTENCIA TECNICA—Technical Assistance). It was set up originally in Guatemala as an espionage cell in 1955 or 1956. Domingo writes: "It seems to have been organized very carefully and was provided with large amounts of capital by Colonel Jaime Rosenberg, a Guatemalan national, former chief of security police of the Arbenz regime, and by a former associate of that same regime. Dr. Ernesto Guevara, an Argentine who later became one of the most important leaders of the 26th of July Movement."

The headquarters of A.T. at first was near CESTA in Cuernavaca. "In the summer of 1956," Domingo writes, "under unknown circumstances, the A.T., which was originally one of the cells of the progressive Guatemalan exiles who wanted to 'liberate' their country from the 'yoke of the lackey of the United States, Colonel Castillo Armas,' was 'turned over' to the leaders of the '26th of July Movement.' (Here, it is appropriate to note, from the very beginning the agents of the A.T. had a surprising interest in Gloria Bolaños, that is, the private secretary and, simultaneously, the intimate friend of Colonel Castillo Armas, who was later assassinated.) Afterwards, the general headquarters of the A.T. was moved to Mexico City, Calle Amparán 49. Nevertheless, 'Ché' Guevara remained in charge of it . . ."

Thus, the rise of "Ché" Guevara to a commanding position within the Castro movement was not accidental. It was the direct result of his role as liaison between the Castro forces and the Soviet network which he partially directed. In the months to come, the A.T., cooperating with such other nets as RAMBLA and DON BASILIO, would provide the Castro forces with invaluable espionage data and with advance information concerning Batista's political decisions, his military plans and the workings of his security and counterintelligence departments. Thus, without giving Castro's movement any visible Communist taint, A.T. would provide a network of agents, cut-outs, mail drops, couriers and sleeper cells; an organization able to collect and evaluate the large amount of intelligence data necessary for successful military action; machinery for safe and secret communications, for the physical movement of undercover agents and for the recruitment of specialists and terrorist elements.

The director of A.T., Ernesto "Ché" Guevara, had been associated with Colonel Jaime Rosenberg, the dreaded chief of security police under the Communist Arbenz regime in Guatemala and the director of its brief, but savage, reign of terror. Guevara was a young Argentine physician, who suffered from asthma, believed fervently in Bolshevik revolutions and had served as a Soviet agent in Guatemala and before that in Peru and Bolivia as well.

(The relationship between "Ché" Guevara and the Soviet apparatuses is not mentioned by either of Castro's sycophantic biographers, Dubois and Brennan. The latter reports: "Ché has denied again and again—so often, in fact, that he becomes morose about it—that he ever was a Communist. The tag was pinned on him because he accepted an appointment in the medical corps of Arbenz' army. Arbenz' throne fell with a clatter in 1954 and Guevara hastened to Mexico City, where he met the Fidelistas.")[10] Critical comment on this analysis would not only be superfluous; it would insult the intelligence of the reader.

[10] Brennan, *op. cit.*, p. 78.

The real brains of A.T., however, was apparently not Guevara, but Hector Cardoza y Aragón, a man of about 60 who remained discreetly in the background, of unknown nationality, the former private secretary of Soviet Ambassador to Mexico Constantine Oumansky. With Roberto Palmero incapacitated by cancer, Cardoza y Aragón was one of the two or three most dangerous and experienced Soviet agents in Latin America.[11]

Another witness on the subject of Fidel Castro and the Soviet underground is Gloria Bolaños, the attractive former secretary and mistress of the late Guatemalan President, Carlos Castillo Armas. In August 1957, a month after the assassination of her lover, Miss Bolaños proceeded to the Dominican Republic. There, she made a lengthy report about Soviet operations in the Caribbean, which stated in part:

"It is, of course, in Mexico that the Communists have established their General Staff or Caribbean command post to direct operations through this part of the world.

"So vast is the cellular labyrinth of the Mexico City bases that a large, expert staff of investigators would be necessary to expose its complexity. It would be found that even at this base the Communists have broken down their organization into self-contained cell units, often unknown to each other."

Adding that President Castillo Armas felt that the main threat to Guatemala came from Mexico City and therefore had the most trusted of his personal intelligence staff attempt to penetrate the Soviet center in Guatemala, Miss Bolaños added that her report was based on material supplied by those agents.

"The 'Ateneo Español' is located at 26 Morelos Avenue, Mexico City. It has the appearance of an ordinary cultural or social club, and does in fact serve as such for thousands of Spanish Republic exiles in Mexico.

"But the 'Ateneo' is also much more. It is one of the most important of the many 'unity' centers of the Caribbean

[11] Domingo, *op. cit.*

Comintern conspiracy. A clearing house for the activities and propaganda of the whole network of Communist-allied forces in this area, the 'Ateneo' also serves as probably the major liaison center between the Caribbean Revolution and International Communism.

"Spanish Republicans, Guatemalans, Dominicans, Venezuelans, Nicaraguans, Peruvians and many others hold endless conferences in this building. It is here that they coordinate the present offensive against what they call 'Yankee imperialism' and against all friends and allies of the United States.

"Matters concerning Fidel Castro and the Cuban Revolution have recently been getting priority even over operations against Guatemala. The series of conferences being held at the Ateneo by Cuban revolutionaries are unceasing.

"The Cuban revolutionary command in Mexico City has a major role in preparing the underground terrorism as well as the military arrangements regarding the revolutionary field forces. Arms, contraband, explosives, training, transportation, propaganda, liaison—all the details of maintaining a growing military force and a terrorist network—are dealt with here."

She then described the "semi-permanent establishment of rented camps, buildings and quarters in the Mexico City area" of the Fidel Castro movement. Summarizing some of the biographical material on Fidel Castro contained in earlier chapters of this book, she concluded that the failure to recognize the Castro movement as "an operation conceived and executed by the Caribbean Comintern" reveals inexcusable "mental paralysis."

This evaluation is dated September 1957, that is to say, nine months after Castro's forces invaded Cuba and 15 months before they triumphed. The realistic and accurate evaluation by the Guatemalan private secretary stands in invidious contrast to the romanticized misrepresentations served to the American public, not merely in 1957, but in

1958 and 1959, by foreign correspondents with world-wide reputations.

To return to the Bolaños report. She noted that "Ché" Guevara "has not hidden the fact that he was a leader of the Juventudes Argentinas Comunistas (the Argentine Communist Youth), that he entered Mexico illegally, and that he is a skilled and experienced military tactician and political terrorist." [12]

Miss Bolaños pointed out that Castro, "until his 1956 invasion of Cuba, had no field military experience of any sort" and added that he "must rely entirely on 'el Ché' for professional advice."

This evaluation would be corroborated by the authoritative British publication, *Intelligence Digest* a year and a half later. Unlike such American publicists as Herbert L. Matthews, Jules Dubois and Edward R. Murrow, the *Intelligence Digest* assessed the Castro movement realistically from the outset.

"Of all the revolutionary groups the Communists have by far the best leadership and the most compact organization," wrote the *Intelligence Digest*. "They are, in fact, the only ones who know exactly what they want.

"This is largely due to the leadership of a somewhat remarkable personality—Dr. Ernesto Guevara, commonly known as "Ché," who is Fidel Castro's chief of staff. The winning of the civil war can be mainly attributed to Guevara. If it had not been for him, Castro would probably still be hiding out in the forests. It was, in fact, only after Guevara took over the effective leadership of the revolutionary movement that success came." [13]

Miss Bolaños added the interesting item that in Mexico

[12] Presumably, Guevara did hide his Communist connections from Ray Brennan and other eulogists of the Castro movement. At least Brennan printed Guevara's denial of his Red connections without giving his readers any indication that it was a lie.
[13] The *Intelligence Digest*, March 1959, Alderbourne Manor, Gerrards Cross, Buchs, England.

Fidel Castro kept in close, but surreptitious, contact with the emigré leadership of Cuban Communism. "In March 1955," she wrote, "Castro moved into apartment 5 of the Mexico Building on No. 5 Insurgentes Norte. By no strange coincidence, the chief of the Cuban C.P., Lazaro Peña, occupied apartment 10 in the same building." [14]

Various conferences were held in Mexico City between the Castro group leadership, the exiled Guatemalan Communists, Hector Aldama, a "former member of the Cuban Maritime Police and extreme leftist, active in a long series of Red-front enterprises" who "put Castro in touch with a number of Peruvian Aprista exiles . . ." Miss Bolaños continued:

"These and other elements met in the residential hotel 'Metropolitan.' It was there that the 26th of July Movement was born . . .

"It was during Mexico City conferences that the Caribbean Comintern recognized Castro as the official champion of the Cuban Revolution." [15]

Like other political groups, the Soviet underground sometimes makes foolish mistakes. At times, men act recklessly and violate security precautions for wholly insufficient reasons. The infallibility, omniscience and omnipotence of the Soviet underground is fortunately a myth. According to *Carib*, one of these strange blunders occurred in Mexico:

"A key figure in the maze of revolutionary organizations in the Caribbean is Hipólito Castillo, who last made one of his rare public appearances in November 1956. He turned up as none other than the commander of the yacht *Gramma* that landed Fidel Castro, 'Ché' Guevara and 80 other revolutionaries in Cuba. He even allowed himself to be photographed for the occasion.[16]

[14] *Carib*, No. 41 (December 1959), pp. 58-65.
[15] *Ibid*, p. 62.
[16] Latin American Communists have a passion for the camera. Many years ago, the writer was shocked and surprised to notice that photographs were being taken in a meeting, obviously secret, of the Central Committee of the Mexican Communist Party.

"This is almost incredible behavior: Hipólito Castillo is one of the top minds in the organizational network in the Caribbean, a veteran activist of the old Comintern and Cominform, and a man sought by a dozen intelligence services." [17]

The reported presence of Castillo on the *Gramma* is not mentioned by Fidel Castro's eulogistic biographers.[18] On the other hand, this is something they would not have been told about by their subject or his entourage. It is improbable that *Carib* would make a mistake in the photographic identification of Hipólito Castillo. The magazine no doubt has a special interest in him since he is a Dominican. We know that Castillo was sent to Mexico in the winter of 1954 in order to create the new top operational command organization of Soviet subversion in Latin America, the *Junta Suprema de Liberación Latinoamericana,* and that he performed this task with signal success.[19]

If *Carib* is correct in stating that Hipólito Castillo was on the *Gramma* as expedition commander, this is further evidence of the great importance which Moscow attached to Fidel Castro's revolutionary project.

[17] *Carib,* No. 23 (March 1959), p. 55.
[18] Jules Dubois, Ray Brennan and Emma and Lidia Castro.
[19] Pedro V. Domingo, "El comunismo en Latinoamerica despues de la liquidacion del Cominform," *Estudios sobre el Comunismo,* Vol. V. No. 15, p. 97, Santiago, Chile. It may be of interest that the names Hipólito Castillo, Roberto Palmero and Hector Cardoza y Aragón, perhaps the three most important Soviet agents in Latin America, do not appear in Robert J. Alexander's *Communism in Latin America,* the book on the subject which the State Department uses to train its Foreign Service personnel assigned to Latin America.

9

From Mexico to the Sierra Maestra

"The fourth group is composed of various ambitious people in the service of the state; and liberals of various shades of opinion. The revolutionaries will pretend to be blindly conspiring with them, obediently following their aims. But we shall do this only the more successfully in order to bring them under our power, *so as to reveal their secrets and completely compromise them.* Thereupon, no path of retreat will be open to them, and they can be used to create disorder within the state."

—Sergei Gennadiyevich
Nechayev
*The Revolutionary
Catechism*[1]

Meanwhile, in Mexico, Castro proceeded to assemble recruits for an armed invasion of Cuba. Their training was under Alberto Bayo, a one-eyed Spaniard born in

[1] Translated by Robert Payne. Emphasis in the original.

Cuba, who served in the Spanish Air Force, helped organize the revolt that overthrew the monarchy and was promoted to Colonel in the Loyalist forces. He was in charge of the expedition against the Balearic Isles, which was a military disaster. After the Loyalist defeat, he emigrated to Mexico, became a Mexican citizen and a powerful figure in the Caribbean Legion. In 1948, he attempted to organize a revolt against President Somoza from Costa Rica. At one time, he was an instructor for the Mexican armed forces, but he was eliminated because he engaged in revolutionary propaganda.[2]

Bayo was characterized in a 1955 Mexican police report as "an international revolutionary with leftist affiliations." On July 11, 1957, Salvador Rivero Martinez, spokesman for the Mexican Nationalist Party, issued a press statement, warning about the danger of Soviet subversion in Mexico. In it, he said: "In Quintano Roo, camps of the Caribbean Brigades —of undisputably Communist origin—have functioned for many years under the command of the Spanish Red, Colonel Alberto Bayo, who is today a naturalized Mexican citizen." Quintano Roo is a wild, malarial and sparsely inhabited border territory of Mexico facing the Caribbean. For years it has served as a corridor both for ordinary smugglers and for Communist agents between Mexico and Central America.

Fidel Castro acquired a ranch near Mexico City, covering 16 miles of mountainous terrain, for the major part of his training operations. Two houses in Mexico City served as headquarters; other buildings were used as arms caches. The trainees were equipped with grenades, bazookas, machine guns, 81 mm. mortars and other infantry weapons. In some undisclosed fashion, they were able to buy Mexican Army issue rifles.

One of the military instructors was Miguel Sánchez, known as el Coreano (the Korean) because he had fought as

---

[2] At this writing (August, 1960) Bayo is organizing in Cuba the "Junta de Liberación Española." It consists mostly of Spanish Loyalist refugees who plan to invade Spain and "liberate" it in the manner of 1936.

a paratrooper in the United States Army during the Korean conflict. He was interviewed at the end of November 1955 by Fidel Castro in Miami and told to proceed to Mexico City at once to train the expeditionary force in the use of modern weapons. In May 1958, el Coreano made a statement about these training operations, which is worth quoting at some length.

El Coreano's "first impression of this group of revolutionaries was excellent." In what appeared to be a jocular tone, Raul Castro said: "So we are to have as an instructor a Yankee invader!" El Coreano replied that the Reds had started the Korean War, not the Americans, and Fidel intervened to state that they should all keep their political convictions to themselves. Nevertheless, el Coreano began to wonder whether "I was going to be part of a rebel army that was going to fight, not for the liberty of Cuba, but as the spearhead of an international Communist thrust."

The first recruits began to arrive in Mexico City in February 1956. "They were, for the most part, young Cubans full of life, ideals and faith—many of them had left behind that which they loved most, mothers, wives, homes, sweethearts: they left everything to give their lives fighting for their country. As these recruits arrived, they were lodged in boarding houses throughout the Federal District, each morning being taken to the firing range of 'Los Gamitos' in the suburb of Santa Fé, near Mexico City—where I had my military instruction center.

"When training commenced, most of the recruits told me of their discontent at having had their passports taken away by Fidel—an act that they considered unjust.[3] As mine had also been taken away, I informed them that they had been seized as a security measure in order that they wouldn't be lost.

[3] Confiscation of the passports of international volunteers is standard operating procedure for the Soviet underground. This was done extensively in Spain. The passports of those who are killed can then be used by Soviet apparatuses to facilitate travel by their agents.

"I received orders from Fidel Castro to watch closely each recruit's behavior, intelligence and physical stamina, etc., *in order that those physically handicapped could be surreptitiously integrated in a special unit to spearhead landings of a more dangerous character.*[4]

"His reason was this: he wanted to make for the mountains with a few highly selected fighters. I told him that it would be inhuman to sacrifice men so full of ideals simply because they were physically weak, furthermore, I respectfully suggested to him that they be used in missions where there was more opportunity of their coming out alive and so be present at the hour of triumph.

"His reply, word by word, was what Napoleon said to Metternich when the latter rebuked him for sacrificing so many thousands of Frenchmen: 'Korean, and what do I care for the lives of a million beings so long as I reach my objective.'

"Continuing, he ordered me to continue the intensive battle training because, for matters of sabotage techniques, he had contracted for a retired Colonel of the Spanish Army, by the surname of Bayo, a veteran instructor of the Red guerrillas in Spain."

El Coreano told his men they would have to fight fiercely in battle, but must be humane to prisoners and the wounded. His statement continues:

"During that period, Raul Castro was a constant visitor to the training camp and was always speaking to the recruits on subjects of a political nature.

"On one of these occasions, he took me aside and told me not to mention so often the practices followed by the U. S. Army in Korea of safeguarding the lives and property of civilians as much as possible. He added that he would fight in a different way in Cuba. It was to be a total war, burning and destroying everything in our path so that the Govern-

[4] My emphasis—N.W.

ment could feel our power and the civilian population would be terrorized into cooperating with us.

"Not being in agreement with this ruthless program of slaughter, I told him: 'By destroying everything in our path, we should only achieve the economic ruin of Cuba and win the hatred of our countrymen. It seems that you are extremely inclined toward Communist tactics, namely, total destruction.

" 'I do not want the historic responsibility of having been the instructor, not of soldiers, but of saboteurs and arsonists.' "

Raul Castro replied: "We have been watching you for some time; you are very Yankee; that little American flag that you have in your apartment is put out of sight very quickly sometimes." El Coreano replied that he could at least display the Cuban flag. "Our only flag is the red and black one of the 26th of July Movement," Raul Castro retorted. Then he added: "We have made a mistake in having an instructor who does not share our views, but you had better watch your step because we are implacable toward the enemies of our system." El Coreano's statement continues:

"An immediate 24-hour watch was kept on my movements, wherever I went I was followed, the house where I lived with my wife and small daughter was also placed under strict surveillance. A couple of days later, a friend of mine, whose name I will not mention since he is still fighting in the 26th of July Movement, told me that Raul Castro and a Spanish sculptor by the surname of Trapote,[5] a Russian NKVD agent in Mexico, were planning my physical elimination. They were deterred only by the fact that my family was with me."

El Coreano wrote to Colonel Alberto Ruiz Novoa, a friend and an anti-Communist and the former commanding officer of the Colombian battalion which fought bravely in

[5] Victor Trapote.

the Korean War. He also wrote an anti-Communist in New York, explaining that he was in danger, that he must leave Mexico promptly and that "my position was deteriorating rapidly." The man in New York had agents in Mexico who were keeping Fidel Castro's movements under surveillance. He advised el Coreano: "to leave the country at the earliest opportunity, giving me his word of honor that my family would be immediately sent to the United States; at the same time he gave me the following instructions: since your passport and those of the group have been impounded by Fidel Castro, the only way to get it back is to volunteer for a dangerous mission abroad."

El Coreano took the matter up with Raul, who said he would consult with Fidel.

"A few days later, I was taken to a meeting where I was strongly rebuked; they said that they doubted very much that I wanted to undertake a dangerous mission, but that nevertheless I could be so assigned if I was willing to leave my wife and daughter with them as hostages. I accepted.

"Before leaving, I had to sign several letters relieving the 26th of July Movement of all responsibility if anything should happen to me.

"Now, in the throes of departure, amidst handshakes and hugs, Fidel and Raul told me that I might do great service to the cause.

"Even as I was leaving, friends were also arranging my family's departure.

"Several days later, I was reunited with my family."

El Coreano was lucky. The Cuban National Police dossier on Fidel Castro has the following entry for 17 October 1956:

"On this date, news was received of the following elements belonging to the 26th of July Movement in Mexico who attempted to desert when they found out about Fidel Castro's Communist leanings and his ties with Alberto Bayo Giraud: Arturo Avalos Marcos and Cirilo Guerra, both of them shot by Fidelistas, reportedly for indiscipline, and Jesus

Bello Melgarejo, a combat veteran of World War II (Cuban by birth, but an American citizen), assassinated in Mexico by the Cuban, Miguel Cabañas Perojo, who stabbed him in the back with a knife under instructions from Fidel Castro."

During 1955-56, Fidel Castro made trips to the United States to raise money for his movement. He addressed meetings in New York, Miami, Tampa and Bridgeport. The official sponsorship of these meetings was usually a committee of the Orthodox Party, but Castro's support was much broader. He appealed to the young, militant, anti-Batista Cubans and to the large colonies of leftwing Latin American exiles. These meetings were opportunities for propaganda; they won volunteers for the military adventure, and they never closed without fervent appeals for funds.

As he had done in the Moncada affair, Fidel Castro claimed that his movement was financed by the collections at these rallies. Such was not the case. A large part of the money came from ex-President Carlos Prio Socarrás in exile in the United States. According to the Cuban National Police dossier on Fidel Castro, Prio told an agent of the Adjutant General's Office of the Cuban Army that he had given Fidel Castro $50,000 to "buy arms and support his people" while in Mexico, through an intermediary named Carlos Maristany. He had also sent Castro two American pilots, named Cross and Mitchell. In return Castro agreed to act jointly with Prio in the revolutionary venture. In the fall of 1956, Prio learned that Fidel Castro had decided to doublecross him and act independently. He had secretly advanced the date of the invasion to cut Prio out of the leadership of the supposedly joint movement. This entry was made in the Castro dossier on November 4, 1956. Twenty-one days later, Prio's fears were realized and Castro's invasion force put out to sea.[6]

Even the laudatory Ray Brennan agrees that Castro got

[6] This item is somewhat ambiguously worded. Hence, it is not clear whether Prio Socarrás deliberately reported Fidel Castro's treachery to the Cuban Army or whether he spoke to a man whom he did not suspect of being a Batista secret agent.

a substantial sum of money from Prio Socarrás. But not through any means as prosaic as an intermediary. According to Brennan, Fidel disguised himself as a laborer, swam the Rio Grande naked, was whisked into a waiting car and brought to a conference with the Cuban ex-President.[7]

On March 14, 1956, the Cuban Police inserted an item in the Fidel Castro dossier, which indicated that their undercover agents in Mexico were functioning efficiently: "During his stay in Mexico, he (Castro) conferred with all leading Cuban Communists and held a number of meetings with Lázaro Peña, Blas Roca, Vicente Lombardo Toledano and the son of Lázaro Cárdenas, all of whom protected him in Mexico. At these interviews, he was accompanied by his brother, Raul Modesto Castro Ruz . . ."[8]

On June 21, 1956, the Mexican Police arrested a group of Fidelista leaders at a meeting. Fidel and five others escaped by car, but were arrested when they got out of the vehicle. The Santa Rosa ranch, 30 kilometers from Mexico City, where Bayo trained the recruits, was also raided and arrests were made there too. Large quantities of arms were seized at both places and the prisoners were charged with carrying firearms without licenses and with possession of contraband weapons.

Passports, training schedules, correspondence and coded communications were seized by the police. The authorities cracked the Castro code without difficulty. As they studied the documents, an interesting picture began to emerge. Complete dossiers were being kept on all recruits, including not only their military training, but their psychic qualities and weaknesses, physical condition, responsiveness to discipline, family and class background, friends and acquaintances. This

---

[7] Brennan, *op. cit.*, p. 95.
[8] Lázaro Peña and Blas Roca are leaders of the Cuban Communist Party. Vicente Lombardo Toledano, the leader of the Latin American Labor Federation (CTAL), is a veteran Soviet agent. Lázaro Cárdenas was President of Mexico in 1934-40. A leftist at that time and not a Communist, he subsequently praised Castro's Cuban dictatorship and accepted the Stalin Peace Prize.

information was backed by long questionnaires which the recruits had to fill out. All of this was standard operating procedure in Communist apparatus organization.

Alice Leone Moats, war correspondent and biographer of Madame Lupescu, was in Mexico City at the time, and wrote an article about the raid and what it disclosed.[9] The daily schedule of the trainees was worked out in minute detail. They were advised that the penalty for betrayal was death. The Mexican police conjectured that the 50 recruits were being trained to serve as officers for a much larger revolutionary force.

"The Director of the Mexican Security Police stated that the objects of the group were to overthrow General Batista by means of a revolution or to assassinate him; and for the latter purpose, they had trained a group of seven individuals in the use of precision rifles fitted with telescopic sights." [10] There was an alternate plan to provide an assassin in Cuba. A letter from an accomplice in Cuba to Fidel Castro was seized which stated, "We will have a volunteer ready to carry the grenade." [11]

Alice Leone Moats wrote that several of the dossiers mentioned prior Communist activities and that at least two of the men arrested were members of the Cuban Young Communist League. "Six days after the arrests were made," she stated, "the police announced that they had uncovered proof that the movement was definitely under the patronage of Communist organizations and inspired by them."

Fidel Castro and his friends were lodged in the Miguel Schultz prison in Mexico City and he was kept there for a month. "During this month, he suffered horribly because he feared that his plan to invade Cuba might fail. They were days of true uncertainty, but thanks to God all these dangers passed." [12]

[9] *National Review,* August 24, 1957.
[10] Fidel Castro dossier.
[11] Moats, *op. cit.*
[12] Emma y Lidia Castro, *op. cit.*, 8th article.

Actually, God had very little to do with it. What saved Fidel Castro from prison or deportation was the vast influence of ex-President Lázaro Cárdenas.[13] On July 25th, the Federal Security Police of Mexico gave Fidel Castro bail so he would be free to try to get a visa to some other country. This was a very lenient approach to the problem, probably a result of the powerful political forces which Castro could activate in Mexico. Fidel and his followers were not merely guilty of illegal possession and carrying of firearms. They had also violated the Mexican immigration laws by entering the country on tourist cards, when they were not tourists, but revolutionaries, and they had violated other laws by training an invasion force against a friendly nation on Mexican soil. If the Mexican authorities had been allowed to let justice take its course, Fidel Castro might still be in a Mexican prison.

Deportation, however, meant the almost certain end of the 26th of July Movement. It was most improbable that another Western Hemisphere country could be found prepared to admit Fidel Castro. If it could, it would probably insist that he abstain from organizing and training invasion forces while on its soil. At the very best, he would have to start all over again. Hence, the entire political power of the Mexican Left had to be exerted to prevent the law from taking its course. We do not know how this pressure was applied, but we do know that it was applied. And it was sufficient.

Fidel Castro and his confederates were released; new arms were purchased; training was resumed. A few months later, Rafael del Pino, Castro's old comrade from the days of the Bogotazo and by now his chauffeur and bodyguard, incurred the homicidal anger of the leader of the expedition. The cause of the quarrel was personal and not, as del Pino would

[13] "That one of the principal people who had to intervene in order that Fidel Castro should not be deported from the country was the ex-President, General Lázaro Cárdenas." Fidel Castro dossier.

later allege, ideological. Castro told friends he was going to kill del Pino that night; these friends warned the bodyguard; del Pino fled in terror, escaping from the ranch and traveling on foot all night until he reached Mexico City.

Top officials of the Cuban Military Intelligence were sent to Mexico. They received detailed information from an informer within the Castro organization. On October 27, 1956, Mexican police raided the house of one of Fidel Castro's female followers. It contained an arsenal.

Invasion

Badly shaken by this second police action, Castro had the arms replaced as completely as possible by purchases on the black market. In November, the insurrectionaries were gradually moved in cars, trucks and buses from Mexico City and its suburbs to Tuxpan, the port of embarkation. On November 25th, Fidel Castro and 82 men set forth on the yacht, *Gramma*, for the invasion of Cuba.

Everything went wrong. Heavy seas and forty-knot gales tossed the small vessel off course. Castro's operational plan had been to synchronize the invasion with an uprising in Santiago, which was to be followed by a revolutionary general strike that was supposed to topple the Batista regime. The rising in Santiago was set for November 30th. Castro and his men were still at sea when they learned by radio that the 26th of July insurrectionaries in that city had managed to free the common criminals from the jails, to burn down police headquarters and to dynamite a warehouse, but that they had been crushed.[14] In Santiago, 20 rebels had been killed and 200 wounded. Batista, remembering Fidel Castro's bloody attack on the Moncada Barracks three years before,

---

[14] Freeing the criminal element so it can take part in the street fighting, looting and arson is a fairly standard tactical measure in Communist uprisings.

suspended civil rights in all provinces except Matanzas and Havana.[15]

The seaborne attempt at invasion was also a disaster. All 82 men managed to land safely at Belic, a small village near Niquero, a few miles west of the towering Sierra Maestra, but the Batista government learned about the operation and deployed troops toward the area. Soon aircraft hit the guerrillas with fragmentation bombs and they were obliged to split into squad-size groups and scuttle for cover. Others surrendered to Cuban Army troops on promise that they would not be mistreated, whereupon, according to Dubois, they were shot.[16]

By mid-December, Fidel Castro reached the Pico Turquino, the highest mountain in Cuba, with 11 survivors of the original invasion force. Ten others had been captured and imprisoned; all the rest had been killed. His group was practically out of ammunition. On the credit side of the ledger, there was the fact that he had some local support from the denizens of the Sierra Maestra. These natives of the region are portrayed, rather naively, by Dubois and other eulogists as poor peasants whose hearts burned with hatred of social injustice. Actually, many of them were fugitives from justice. Some were professional smugglers; others had been involved in narcotics, criminal frauds and various other offenses. They were naturally against the government and potential recruits for any destructive adventure. However, Castro had no arms to give them. Decades earlier, Stalin had spoken admiringly of "the bold world of bandits" and had called them "the only true revolutionaries."

On arrival at the Sierra Maestra, Castro found a ranch foreman who was accused of making false charges against

[15] Dubois, *op. cit.*, pp. 138-40. On straight factual matters where Castro and his propagandists had no reason to want to lie to him, Dubois is a reliable source.

[16] *Ibid*, p. 143. The writer has no idea whether this statement is true or false.

peasants and cheating them out of their land. In true Chinese Communist style, he haled this wretched creature before a kangaroo court, convicted him and had him shot.

Lost in admiration of this lynching, reporter Dubois wrote: "Thus Castro was to become the Robin Hood of the Sierra Maestra and was to pursue later the same policy of taking from the rich to give to the poor." [17]

Castro had only a handful of men. But there were several advantages he could count upon. The first was the predictable negligence and corruption of the Batista dictatorship and its military leadership. Perhaps the worst sort of military dictator is a soldier who knows practically nothing about strategy and tactics.

His second advantage was the support of the vast, submerged Soviet apparatus I have already described and the enthusiasm his movement generated among the youth of Cuba. As for the Cuban people in general, the reaction was one of apathy and antagonism to Castro's revolution. Ruby Hart Phillips, soon to become a zealous supporter of the 26th of July Movement, reported as follows on the state of public opinion:

"In Havana, news of the Castro expedition stirred little interest among the general public. It was considered merely another hare-brained scheme, like the suicidal attack on the Moncada post in 1953. Commerce and industry were prospering, the tourist season was good, the government was pouring millions into public works and new industry. The Capital hoped the government would crush the tiny rebellion without loss of time." [18]

The third advantage which Castro had was the fanatical support of a clique of foreign correspondents, of whom the most important was Herbert L. Matthews of the *New York Times*. A month or two after the Castro invasion, Matthews

[17] *Ibid,* p. 145.
[18] Phillips, *op. cit.,* p. 291.

decided to go to Cuba with his wife and so informed the NBC correspondent in Havana, Ted Scott.[19] At this juncture, Castro sent an emissary to Havana to ask that an American correspondent go into the Sierra Maestra and interview him. This would be a sensational news scoop since the United Press had reported that Castro was dead.[20] The emissary was Faustino Pérez. He was a Communist,[21] but naturally Mrs. Phillips did not know that.

As Mrs. Phillips tells the story, Matthews was the logical man to go to the Sierra Maestra because it was a "one-shot" assignment. That is to say, there was a strong possibility that Batista would expel from Cuba any newspaperman who interviewed Castro. This excluded reporters stationed in Cuba, but not the roving Matthews.

This version, however, is contradicted by Ambassador Gardner. He states that Matthews pleaded with him to get Batista's permission for the trip to the Sierra Maestra and the Castro interview. Gardner got Batista's approval, he states, but made Matthews promise to report to him on the meeting with Castro. The Ambassador adds that Matthews welched on his part of the bargain. Thus, the Matthews trip was not high adventure, but a journey so arranged as to eliminate any element of personal danger.

Matthews got through to the Sierra Maestra and interviewed Castro. His articles in the *New York Times*, published in late February 1957, "had tremendous impact, not only on Cuba, but on the entire hemisphere."[22] In a sense, this was not reporting, but propaganda and moral exhortation of the most skillful sort. A veteran in the game of making Communist-dominated movements appear as crusades for democracy and freedom—as, for example, in Spain

[19] *Ibid*, p. 298.
[20] The Batista government could have avoided this scoop very simply: by denying that Castro had been killed, but adding that his movement was insignificant.
[21] BRAC Report, *op. cit.*
[22] Phillips, *op. cit.*, p. 290.

at the time of the Civil War—Herbert Matthews built up Castro as a hero, pleaded for him as a downtrodden underdog, gave eschatological assurance of final victory.

"As I learned later," Matthews wrote, "Señor Castro was waiting until he had his forces reorganized and strengthened and had mastery of the Sierra Maestra" before consenting to see the world press. Did he have mastery of the Sierra Maestra at the time as Matthews claimed? It seems most doubtful.

Matthews said that Castro had been fighting for 79 days and was steadily gaining in strength. Then the appeal to underdoggery. He quoted Castro as telling him:

"Batista has 3,000 men in the field against us. I will not tell you how many we have for obvious reasons. He works in columns of 200; we in groups of 10 to 40, and we are winning."

Then hero worship: "The personality of the man is overpowering. It was easy to see that his men adored him and also to see why he has caught the imagination of the youth of Cuba all over the island. Here was an educated, dedicated fanatic, a man of ideals, of courage and of remarkable qualities of leadership."

And in his second article, published February 25th, Matthews gave the American people the assurance that they would insist on before accepting anyone as a fighter for human freedom. He wrote: "there is no communism to speak of in Fidel Castro's 26th of July Movement . . ."

Former U.S. Ambassador to Cuba Earl E. T. Smith testified as follows on August 30, 1960 concerning the influence of Herbert Matthews and his articles on American policy toward Cuba:

MR. SMITH. I have been asked many times what part if any the United States played in Castro and Communist rise to power in Cuba. The U.S. Government agencies and the U.S. press played a major role in bringing Castro to power.

"Three front-page articles in the *New York Times* in early

1957, written by the editorialist Herbert Matthews, served to inflate Castro to world stature and world recognition. Until that time, Castro had been just another bandit in the Oriente Mountains of Cuba, with a handful of followers who had terrorized the campesinos, that is the peasants, throughout the countryside.

"Fidel Castro landed on the south coast of Oriente in December of 1956 from Mexico with an expeditionary force of 81 men. Intercepted by Cuban gunboats and patrol planes, Castro and a handful of stragglers managed to ensconce themselves in the rugged 8,000-foot Sierra Maestra Range.

"After the Matthews articles which followed an exclusive interview by the *Times* editorial writer in Castro's mountain hideout and which likened him to Abraham Lincoln, he was able to get followers and funds in Cuba and in the United States. From that time on arms, money and soldiers of fortune abounded. Much of the American press began to picture Castro as a political Robin Hood.

"Also because Batista was the dictator who unlawfully seized power, American people assumed Castro must, on the other hand, represent liberty and democracy. The crusader role which the press and radio bestowed on the bearded rebel blinded the people to the leftwing political philosophy with which even at that time he was already on record.

"His speeches as a student leader, his interviews as an exile while in Mexico, Costa Rica, and elsewhere clearly outlined a Marxist trend of political thought.

"The official U.S. attitude toward Castro could not help but be influenced by the pro-Castro press and radio; certain Members of Congress picked up the torch for him. . . .

"There were a number of times, number of occasions when I was asked as the Ambassador if we would help the church in its efforts to establish a bridge between Castro and Batista, or if we, in any way, would support a national unity government. Such government would act as a provisional government in Cuba to maintain law and order while elections were being held.

"The United States would never agree to support or would never permit me to negotiate, because it would be considered as intervening in the internal affairs of Cuba."

Ambassador Smith added:

"I would say that Mr. Wieland [23] and all those who had anything to do with Cuba had a close connection with Herbert Matthews.

"I will go further than that. I will say that when I was Ambassador, that I was thoroughly aware of this, and sometimes made the remark in my own Embassy that Mr. Matthews was more familiar with the State Department thinking regarding Cuba than I was." [24]

[23] William Arthur Wieland, Director of the Caribbean Division, Central American Affairs, Department of State.
[24] Senate Internal Security Subcommittee, *Communist Threat to the United States Through the Caribbean, Hearings,* Part 9, August 27, 30, 1960, pp. 685-7.

10

The Conquest of Power

"The passion for destruction is a creative passion."
—Mikhail Bakunin

IN 1934, Stalin had a momentous conversation with the French Communist writer, Henri Barbusse, in which he said that Latin America was at a stage of social development comparable to that of China. Therefore, the Chinese, rather than the Russian, revolution should be the model for the Latin parties. In accordance with this decision, Eudocio Ravines, a Peruvian revolutionist and one of the most important figures in Latin American Communism, was instructed to spend several days in conversation with Mao Tse-tung and other Chinese Communist leaders who were in Moscow at the time. He was thoroughly indoctrinated by them in the modus operandi of the Chinese Communist road to power and its application to Latin America. All this is told in detail in *The Yenan Way,* the brilliant and important book which Ravines published in 1951 after his break with Communism.[1]

Despite Stalin's decision that China should be the model for Latin American Communism, all Communist-led armed

[1] Charles Scribner's Sons, New York.

insurrections in the Western Hemisphere continued to be based on the Russian model of October 1917. That is to say, they were sudden, concentrated blows directed at the great cities, designed to seize the nerve ganglia of power by means of speed, surprise and massive impact. They were urban insurrections. Their striking force was an urban group: theoretically the working class; actually, more frequently the radical middle class and students. The model for these insurrections was taken from Heinz Neumann's classic text, *The Armed Insurrection of the Proletariat*. Neumann was the real leader of the German Communist Party before Hitler took power. Thus, the design was not only Russian, but German as well. (Fidel Castro's attack on the Moncada Barracks in 1953 suggests that he may have studied Neumann's book, which had been translated into Spanish and was studied by many Latin American revolutionaries, even though the application and planning were faulty.)

The Chinese road to power was very different. Defeated in their efforts to seize power in the great cities and hold that power against the Nationalist forces of Chiang Kai-shek, the Communists made their "long march" into the primitive hinterland. Here Mao Tse-tung built a rival, enclave state and defended and expanded it by means of guerrilla tactics. In a military sense, the Yenan Way was gradual and erosive, whereas the Petrograd Way was a sudden explosion of violence. The Yenan Way was to develop a base of operations at the periphery and gradually accumulate enough strength to attack the core. By contrast, the Petrograd Way was to seize the hub, then expand outward to subdue the hinterland. The Yenan Way relied on the peasantry; the Petrograd Way on the urban working class.

From a military standpoint, the Fidel Castro insurrection, which began in the remote, primitive and difficult Sierra Maestra, was the first Latin American application of the Chinese Communist strategy of the struggle for power. This was not the original intention. Castro had planned to synchronize his landing with the urban uprising in Santiago and to attack the city of Manzanilla and capture it, then to advance toward Havana. All of this miscarried. Nevertheless the success of Castro's military operation, contrasted with the many Latin American Petrograd-type insurrections which failed, will probably tend to make the Yenan Way dominant in future Latin revolutions led by Communists.

The Miracle of the Sierra Maestra

The picture which Herbert L. Matthews and other Castro propagandists would give the world was one of a gallant, ill-armed, impoverished, outnumbered band that defeated the armies of Batista because their cause was just and their hearts were pure. This version appealed to the incorrigibly moralistic streak in the American mind, but it was a travesty of the truth.

Fidel Castro's forces won primarily because they had almost unlimited supplies of money. The implication in Dubois' book and similar sources that the movement was financed primarily by small contributions raised by Castro's Civic Resistance organizations in Havana and elsewhere is just silly.[2] Civil wars cost money, money in vast quantities. The sources for such funds are almost always governments, occasionally men of great wealth, almost never the nickels and dimes contributed by faithful followers.

"The first bitter pill was the revelation that Fidel was not the brave military hero his highly-paid public relations campaign made him to be," wrote Stanley Ross, the editor of *el Diario de Nueva York*, "In fact, he never won a battle, much less the war." Then Ross added:

"Fidel's secret weapon was money—incredible millions of dollars, with which he bought 'victories.' He bought entire regiments from Batista's officers and, on one occasion,

[2] Dubois, *op. cit.*, p. 249.

purchased for $650,000 cash an entire armored train, with tanks, guns, ammunition, jeeps and 500 men." [3]

According to Ross, Fidel Castro received $50 million from Venezuela alone "plus many millions in 'taxes' on the sugar planters and Cuban industrialists while he was staging the revolution." The Venezuela referred to is the Democratic Action regime of Castro's old friend from Bogotazo days, President Rómulo Betancourt.

There is no dispute whatsoever about the powerful support which Betancourt gave the 26th of July Movement. The real question is whether the Venezuelan knew from the outset that it was Communist-dominated. Betancourt has pursued much more moderate policies than Castro in Venezuela, has welcomed United States private investment and has refrained from denunciations of the United States. However, Venezuela is not Cuba. If Betancourt attempted Castro policies in Caracas, informed Latin Americans maintain, he would be deposed by the Venezuelan Army.

There is other evidence that Castro's forces floated to victory on a sea of loot. Martin and Santora wrote:

"And there was plenty of money.

" 'Once,' said a man who was close to Fidel, 'Carlos Rafael Rodriguez, an active member of the Communist Party in Cuba,[4] arrived with a dozen men loaded with money. It came to $800,000 and Fidel hugged him and shouted, "Now we're ready to win the war." ' " [5]

One year after Fidel Castro's landing in the Oriente the *Intelligence Digest* of London reported that the 26th of July Movement was led by Communists and was part of a

---

[3] Stanley Ross, "We Were Wrong About Castro," *American Weekly,* June 12, 1960, pp. 4-5. The word "we" in the title is significant. *El Diario de Nueva York* supported Castro at first, then quickly discovered his movement was Communist and opposed him.

[4] It would be more accurate to call him the brains of the Communist Party and its most influential leader.

[5] Martin and Santora, *op. cit.,* 3rd article.

Communist conspiracy to seize power in the Caribbean that was lavishly financed from behind the Iron Curtain. The *Digest* reported:

"Fidel Castro's rebel organization has the financial and arms support of the Soviet Union and Communist groups throughout the western hemisphere.

"The preparation of this coup alone cost Communist sources a very large sum of money, of which only a small part came from the former President, Carlos Prio Socarrás. The bulk of it came from Russian and Chinese subsidies, channeled through secret groups in several Latin American countries, including Costa Rica, Chile and Argentina. Since the beginning of the revolt, these funds have poured into Cuba and are financing not only the operations in Oriente Province, but also subversive activities in other parts of the island."

In his testimony before a Senate Subcommittee on August 30, 1960, former Ambassador Earl E. T. Smith mentioned other sources of funds and arms at Castro's disposal. Ex-President of Cuba Carlos Prío Socarrás "was operating out of the United States, out of Florida, supplying the revolutionaries with arms, ammunition, bodies and money. Batista told me that when Prío left Cuba, Prío and Alameia took $140 million out of Cuba. If we cut that estimate in half, they may have shared $70 million. It is believed that Prío spent a great many millions of dollars in the United States assisting the revolutionaries. This was done right from our shores."

According to Smith, about ten shipments of contraband arms got through to Castro for every one that was seized. "We refused to sell arms to a friendly government," he testified, "and we persuaded other friendly governments not to sell arms to Cuba. Yet, on the other hand revolutionary sympathizers were delivering arms, bodies and ammunition daily from the United States. We were lax in enforcing our neutrality laws."

Former Ambassador Gardner confirmed this shameful

story of covert United States intervention to undermine the legitimate Cuban government by conniving at violations of American law. He pointed out that Prío Socarrás "was arrested, convicted, and paid a fine of $5,000 for gunrunning." He was indicted a second time, but nothing was ever done about it.

Once it was becoming clear that the pseudo-liberals in the State Department were committed to engineering a Castro victory, Fidel attempted to extort tribute from American business firms in Cuba. With State Department approval, Ambassador Smith wrote U.S. firms on the island telling them not to submit to this sort of blackmail. However, by the closing months of the Batista era, American firms were buying protection from the guerrilla forces.

"There is evidence that during August, Russian submarines twice surfaced off Cuba and discharged munitions for Castro's forces." [6]

Whenever he had a choice, Fidel Castro took Russian money in preference to Free World money. In June, 1960, a 24-page memorandum on Cuban-Communist ties was released in Mexico City by Justo Carrillo Hernandez, formerly President of Cuba's Economic Development Bank and the most important Castro official who had defected up to that time.[7] According to the *Washington Post* of June 16, 1960:

"Carrillo also disclosed that early in 1959 he and other Cuban government bankers had worked out with international credit agencies[8] and firms a full-scale plan to finance the Cuban revolution. But Castro scuttled the plan and, added Carrillo, 'Cuba was sold to Russian Communism for rubles.'"

Castro used the huge funds at his disposal to buy peasant support, to scour world markets for arms and to suborn

[6] The *Intelligence Digest,* edited by Kenneth de Courcy, London, December 1957.
[7] In late 1958, Castro considered Carrillo for the post of provisional President of Cuba.
[8] Primarily, the International Monetary Fund.

Batista's army. One of the reasons Castro was able to buy treason among Cuban military leaders was that Batista had already largely demoralized them.

Batista as Wrecker

As a young man, Batista had been associated with an anarchist group called *Germinación*. Before his sergeants' revolt, he had had close associations with Communist groups among the tobacco workers. His general attitude was antimilitary and, as I pointed out in an earlier chapter, his coup d'etat in the 1930's helped demoralize the Cuban armed forces and strip the officer class of authority.[9] When he took power a second time in 1952, one of his first acts was to dismiss the top military commanders of the Cuban armed forces and substitute his own henchmen.

He saw himself as a national political leader not as a military dictator. "The one dream Batista always entertained was to enjoy popularity with the people of Cuba," wrote Dubois, who hated him.[10] And Ruby Hart Phillips, a more unbiased observer, thought: "Although General Batista rose to power as a strong man, he would prefer to be the ruler by popular acclaim. His close friends say he has little liking for military trappings." [11]

His second round in power was an era of flagrant corruption. Dubois wrote: "Señora Batista was receiving fifty percent of the profits of the slot machines in the gambling casinos that Batista had allowed to be opened throughout the country. Army and police officers and some naval officers were also profiting from this system of official corruption. Batista was receiving his take through intermediaries, and

[9] Right after his first coup d'etat, Batista wired one of his sergeant co-conspirators, promoting him to a captaincy. Too late, was the reply, "I already promoted myself to colonel." Dubois, *op. cit.*, p. 12.
[10] *Ibid*, p. 156.
[11] *New York Times*, August 2, 1953.

some of the money was being used to buy off army officers and politicians." [12]

In short, Batista had corrupted the military leadership of the nation and given it an example of corruption in the presidency. This suited the Soviets. They had more money and they were playing for higher stakes.

In addition to the regular forces fighting Castro and selling out to him, there was a private army—the so-called *Tigres* of Senator Rolando Masferrer. In the Spanish Civil War, Masferrer had been a Communist and had seen how terror is organized and applied on a huge scale. He had been at least an observer of OGPU liquidations of Anarchists, Socialists and other leftwing Spaniards who opposed Stalin. In time, Masferrer broke with the Communist movement, but not with its methods. In mid-1958, he organized his private army of "tigers" in the Oriente which committed outrages against the civilian population. While combatting Castro, it was also driving decent elements of the population into the Castro movement.

Batista was not a dictator in the European sense of the word. He was a *caudillo*, a politician who balanced forces, a man who no more wielded total power than a Chinese war lord. In early 1958, Batista ordered private individuals to "leave the suppression of terroristic activities to the armed forces." Masferrer felt strong enough in the Oriente to ignore the order. Ruby Hart Phillips observed that the Masferrer private army of about 1,500 men was "the scourge of Oriente Province, robbing, killing, torturing and extorting money." [13]

The regular armed forces and the police contributed their share to killing prisoners after they had surrendered and to shooting down teen-agers suspected of terrorism and leaving their corpses on the streets as a warning. Some of these re-

[12] Dubois, *op. cit.*, p. 157.
[13] Phillips, *op. cit.*, pp. 318-9.

prisals were savage enough to turn the stomachs of men of good will and thus strengthen Castro's support among the population.

Later, Castro would pound into the ears of the Cuban people the charge that Batista's government had 20,000 corpses on its conscience. This is dismissed by responsible observers as propaganda. Its purpose was to destroy the prestige of the Cuban Army and prepare the nation psychologically for its physical extermination by revolutionary terror. Annihilation of professional armies and their replacement by Red workers' battalions is, as Lenin pointed out, a vital precondition to the consolidation of Soviet dictatorship.

The Martian Women

The Castro forces were brilliant propaganda strategists and they knew how to utilize the conduct of the Cuban armed forces and of the *Tigres* to win public sympathy. In early 1958, General Alberto Bayo, the Spanish Communist who had trained Fidel Castro's forces, sent Castro a letter of instructions. It was taken to Cuba by an American newspaper correspondent, but a microfilmed copy of it fell into the hands of the Cuban authorities. The document in my possession is a paraphrase;[14] Martin and Santora apparently had access to the actual microfilm.[15] Both are the same in essence and evidently authentic since they agree generally with the recommendations made by Bayo in his book on guerrilla strategy and tactics.[16] I quote from Martin and Santora's version:

"Start activating a program of agitation on a large scale to encompass the most important cities [in Cuba]. Begin with your active groups to terrorize the population, using bombs,

---

[14] BRAC report.
[15] Martin and Santora, 3rd article. They are able to date the letter March 8, 1958, which the BRAC report does not do.
[16] Bayo, *op. cit.*

petards (stink bombs), Molotov cocktails, lighted matches in public vehicles, etc.

"If this fails, or if you see that the people don't respond, begin a wave of sabotage aimed in particular against the sugar centers of the interior. If this also fails, then start with personal attempts on the lives of individuals belonging to the armed forces and the police.

'Endeavor to use for this task minors, because the police are scared of being tough with them for fear of public criticism. When this happens use written propaganda. Have the women in your group wear black dresses to impress the people further—this always gives a good result." [17]

This cynical advice to spread terror, create teen-age martyrs and organize demonstrations of phony widows was superfluous. Fidel Castro had already put most of it into practice and in a dramatic fashion that gripped the imagination of the American people.

In June 1957, the United States recalled Ambassador Arthur Gardner because he had been branded as a close friend and open admirer of Batista. Earl E. T. Smith, a broker and a friend of Gardner, was given the post. Ambassador Smith's instructions were to counteract the reportedly pro-Batista attitude of his predecessor. On July 31st, against the advice of experienced Cuban liberals who feared that the Castro movement would exploit his presence there, Smith went to Santiago.

The 26th of July propaganda machine went into action. A group, which called itself the "Martian Women," had been organized under Dr. Martha Frade Barraque, a Communist, who would later be rewarded by being put in charge of health and social welfare by the Castro government. These women put on widow's weeds and staged a demonstration in front of Ambassador Smith. Although most of them were not mothers, they carried a banner which read "STOP KILLING OUR SONS."

[17] Martin and Santora, *op. cit.*, 3rd article.

With the stupidity which characterized much of its action, the Batista police in Santiago turned fire hoses on the women and some of them were handled brutally. Ambassador Smith was immediately queried by the press concerning the demonstration and the police action. He stated that he was disturbed that his presence in Santiago should be used as the occasion for a demonstration against the government to which he was accredited. He was asked whether he approved of police brutality and replied that there would be a press conference later. He talked to two assistants, held the conference, repeated his first statement and added that he abhorred police brutality.

This addition was what the newspaper men wanted to hear. It was this that made the world headlines. Although Ambassador Smith knew that the Castro movement was Communist-infiltrated and dangerous to United States interests, although he had spoken at Santiago with great caution precisely to avoid conveying the impression that the United States sided with the rebels, this was exactly the interpretation which the "liberal" American reporters put on his words. "Smith was horrified by the brutality and it shocked his wife, who was also in the automobile," wrote Jules Dubois, adding that Ambassador Smith's statement "criticized the employment of police brutality in any form." [18] Dubois failed to mention that the American Ambassador also resented having his presence exploited by Castro and the Communists.

The Soviet Submarines

The United States press gave full and romantic coverage to the Castro story. It went into emotional orgies about the bullet-riddled corpses of teen-age Cuban boys, forgetting to add that these same boys spread terror with Molotov cocktails and booby traps, skulked in the dark to waylay and

[18] Dubois, *op. cit.*, p. 173.

butcher individual soldiers and policemen, and took part in the so-called revolutionary tribunals which sentenced peasants to death for refusing to have anything to do with Castro's treasonable movement.

The American press was, on the whole, mute on another interesting point. Where did Castro get his arms? The *Intelligence Digest*, one of the few publications which was consistently right about the true character of the Castro movement, reported after its triumph:

"Right up to the end of the civil war, Batista had greater public support than Fidel Castro. Castro won because he made the greatest possible use of the guerrilla tactics taught to him by Dr. Guevara; whereas the police and Batista's army functioned as regular forces trying to limit the destruction and to protect life and property. They proved unable to cope with guerrilla tactics ably carried out. Castro, therefore, was able to ruin the country's economy and thus to bring about the collapse of Batista's regime.

"During the last months of the war, Castro's forces had by far the most modern weapons and a seemingly inexhaustible supply of ammunition. He also had large funds at his disposal.

"Castro had Czech and Russian weapons. His brother, Raul, made several trips behind the Iron Curtain on fundraising missions and to arrange supplies of arms. This is always officially denied—nevertheless it is true. It is, in fact, absolutely unthinkable that Castro could have carried out so extensive a campaign without considerable support from a foreign Government, and there is no doubt as to which Government that was. The suggestion that his funds came from private sources can be entirely excluded." [19]

This analysis was confirmed by other sources. On November 26, 1958, two Fidelistas were wounded badly in a firefight with Havana police, turned themselves in to a city hospital and were interrogated the next day by SIM agents.

[19] March 1959.

Their names were Eduardo Valdivia and Ramiro Sanchez. They stated that, while serving with Raul Castro's forces, their units had received a large shipment of modern arms delivered by a submarine of unknown nationality.

They added that a uniformed man, known as Agapito Venereo, disembarked from the submarine, was greeted warmly by veteran revolutionaries, then, to their astonishment, was ordered seized and almost instantly executed. The submarine landed arms at La Chiva, Nipe Bay, Oriente Province. Veteran 26th of July fighters told them that La Chiva had been used for decades "in the cause of the Revolution" as a training area, regional headquarters and port of embarkation. It had played a role in the 1930 revolutionary disturbances and in the Caribbean Legion invasion attempts of the mid-1940's.[20]

This report was corroborated on July 14, 1959, by the testimony before a United States Senate Commitee of Major Pedro L. Diaz Lanz, the Chief of the Cuban Air Force who defected when he discovered the Castro movement was Communist-dominated. Major Diaz Lanz stated under oath:

"In the first days of January (1958), I had information of a submarine close to the north shore of Cuba. Also during the time I was sick, a friend of mine who did work with me in the underground in Santiago, Cuba; a very dependable man, very serious, he told me he saw on the north shore of the Oriente Province during the time Raul Castro was controlling that zone . . . a submarine close to the shore.

"Chairman EASTLAND. That was in the north zone.

"Major DIAZ. North zone, yes. And he saw strange people and he told me they wasn't speaking English or French or something like that. They were speaking Russian." [21]

Diaz Lanz added that his friend was sure that the sub-

[20] *Carib,* #37 (October 1959), pp. 11-12.
[21] Senate Internal Security Subcommittee, *Communist Threat to the United States Through the Caribbean,* Part 1, 1959, p. 15.

marine and crew were Russian, that the crew wore naval uniforms of a type he had never before seen and that the supplies were of vital importance to Raul Castro because he had a large number of troops and was getting very little arms from his brother.

Castro, the Warrior

Reporters Martin and Santora collected very interesting eyewitness accounts of the conduct of the Robin Hood of the Sierra Maestra. These are almost completely at variance with the romantic portrayals disseminated by such shapers of American public opinion as Edward R. Murrow of CBS and Herbert L. Matthews of the *New York Times*.

One man who was with Fidel Castro in the Sierra Maestra had this to say:

"Even after I knew he was a physical coward, a glutton and a tool of the Reds, I stuck with him in the hope he would be content to sit back and allow a man with character to run the government . . .

"He had a high-powered rifle with a telescopic sight and he would aim it down a mountainside, fire it a couple of times and shout—like a child 'I got him. I got him.' We never found the body of the so-called victim.

"He sent us to fight, but he rarely fought himself. He acted like a scared man underneath the bravado. He used men as carelessly as he used bullets for his rifle. He was a pitiless, two-faced man who cursed his followers and took away any dignity they might have had, and even sacrificed them for propaganda purposes.

"I remember vividly one man who was Castro's personal professional killer. He obeyed orders without question. At the time, Castro's popularity was waning with the local farmers, whose support he needed. He had to do something spectacular to show them he was a friend.

"A mountain girl became pregnant and Castro accused

his pet assassin of having a romance with her. We all knew it was someone else, but that made no difference. He had the man tried and executed. In this way, he showed the farmers he would kill his boys if they got out of line." [22]

When the guerrilla forces were on the move, Fidel would remind his men not to forget his cognac. He would take benzedrine pills with a brandy chaser. He ate gluttonously, wiping his mouth on his sleeve. "Occasionally, he received a shipment of caviar and would gorge himself. Cigars were flown in by helicopter." [23] These luxuries were supplied by the Batista general, Eulogio Cantillo, who had either sold out to Castro or was trying to be in the good graces of whichever *caudillo* won. The cognac, caviar and cigars arrived in a Cuban Air Force helicopter.

"The Castro forces themselves never won a military victory," Ambassador Smith testified. The basic reason for the defeat of Batista's armies, he asserted, was that covert United States intervention shattered their morale.

"Primarily I would say that when we refused to sell arms to the Cuban Government and also by what I termed intervening by innuendo (which was persuading other friendly governments not to sell arms to Cuba) that these actions had a moral, psychological effect upon the Cuban armed forces which was demoralizing to the nth degree.

"The reverse, it built up the morale of the revolutionary forces. Obviously when we refused to sell arms to a friendly government, the existing government, the people of Cuba and the armed forces knew that the United States no longer would support Batista's government.

"A decision such as prohibiting the sale of arms to a friendly nation can have devastating effects upon the government in power.

"We even did not fulfill our promise to deliver 15 training planes, which had been bought and paid for by the Batista

[22] Martin and Santora, *op. cit.,* 3rd article.
[23] *Ibid.*

government. In accordance with instructions from the State Department I informed Batista that delivery would be suspended, because we feared some harm might come to the 47 kidnaped Americans. The kidnaping by Raul Castro of 30 U.S. marines and sailors, 17 American citizens, and 3 Canadians occurred at this time.

"After the kidnaped Americans were returned we still refused to deliver these training planes because we feared that bombs could be put on the planes even though they were strictly for training purposes.

"I reiterate that decisions such as these may determine whether a government can remain in power.

"Although they could buy arms and ammunition from other sources, the psychological impact on the morale of the government was crippling. On the other hand, it gave a great uplift to the morale of the rebels."

Former Ambassador Gardner declared that a shipment of military equipment to Batista, arranged under the mutual aid pact, was "stopped" on the New York docks. He declared it was "common gossip" that "Rubottom was the only man who could have stopped it."

Thus, the war in the Sierra Maestra was a sordid struggle, conducted by means of bribery, lies and betrayal. Neither of the two protagonists was fit to govern any people or any nation. Where Batista was merely avid for applause, greedy and corrupt, Castro had far more terrible vices. He was a psychopath, devoid of any morality or honor, dedicated to nihilism and to naked power.

Both men had murky social origins and the rebelliousness, envy and hostility often characteristic of the underdog. The losers in the civil war of the Sierra Maestra were those Cubans who were well educated, dedicated to their country, honorable and idealistic, in short, what Jefferson once called "the natural aristocracy of intellect and morals." Some of these men died because they were officials and hence fair prey for Castro's terrorists; others were career officers who died in battle or else were shot against the wall later for having refused to be traitors; still others were men who supported Batista, despite revulsion, because they knew Communism was far worse.

On the other side, there were the legions of young men and women, generally from good families, well-educated, highly intelligent and visionary, who fought for Castro because they thought he stood for freedom. Some died in the conflict; thousands of others were imprisoned or shot after the victory because they would not accept Communist dictatorship.

Many share the blood guilt for the needless death of these people, who were the best element in Cuba. Among the guilty are American correspondents who, either willfully or because of slackness and incompetence, wrote falsehoods about the Castro movement so other people would fight and die for it.

11

The Blind Colossus

"It has been said that the character of the philosophy of the eighteenth century was a sort of adoration of human intellect, an unlimited confidence in its power to transform at will laws, institutions, customs. To be accurate, it must be said that the human intellect which some of these philosophers adored was simply their own. They showed, in fact, an uncommon want of faith in the wisdom of the masses. I could mention several who despised the public almost as heartily as they despised the Deity. Toward the latter they evinced the pride of rivals —the former they treated with pride of parvenus. They were as far from real and respectful submission to the will of the majority as from submission to the will of God. Nearly all subsequent revolutionaries

have borne the same char-
acter. Very different from
this is the respect shown by
Englishmen and Americans
for the sentiments of the
majority of their fellow
citizens. Their intellect is
proud and self-reliant, but
never insolent; and it has
led to liberty, while ours
has done little but invent
new forms of servitude."
—Alexis de Tocqueville
*The Old Regime and
the French Revolution*[1]

U NDER AMBASSADOR GARDNER, United States policy favored the Batista regime and the American Embassy in
Havana warned the State Department concerning Communist infiltration of the Castro movement. Until the spring of
1958, the Cuban Government was allowed to purchase arms
from the United States and these arms were naturally used
against the insurrectionaries. It had for a long time been a
standing policy of the United States to give anti-Communist
governments in Latin America the military aid needed to
combat external or internal attempts at Communist subversion.

In and around the State Department, there were powerful
men, whose tendency was ultra "liberal," who believed that
Batista, and not Communism, was the chief threat to the
welfare and security of the Hemisphere, and who supported
the Castro movement as a cleansing, progressive force. In

[1] Doubleday and Company, Garden City, 1955. Translated by Stuart Gilbert.
Reprinted in *The Intellectuals*, George B. de Huszar (editor), Free Press,
Glencoe, Ill., 1960, p. 13.

Congress, Representative Charles O. Porter as well as Senator Wayne Morse were two early and influential supporters of Castro. To a lesser extent, so was Representative Adam Clayton Powell, a Harlem racist and demagogue with a voting record that revealed interesting parallels with the Communist Party line. The American Republics Subcommittee of the Senate Foreign Affairs Committee was dominated by the energetic and scholarly Senator Wayne Morse of Oregon, a former Republican turned Democrat, who had become a spokesman for the Americans for Democratic Action.

Of these men, Representative Charles O. Porter of the 4th District of Oregon was without doubt the most vocal and influential supporter of the suicidal view that the United States should support leftwing and socialist regimes throughout Latin America and that Fidel Castro was the champion of a "people's" revolution. Early in 1959, a Boston stockbroker wrote to his Congressman, Laurence Curtis, questioning the wisdom of allowing Castro to come to the United States and address colleges and other groups in view of his alleged Communist background. Congressman Curtis replied that he was turning the letter over to Representative Charles O. Porter "because as a member of the House Foreign Relations Committee he has a particular interest in that area."

Porter's reply to Curtis contained this paragraph: "No one in the State Department believes Castro is a Communist, or a Communist sympathizer, nor does any other responsible person who wants to get his facts straight." This letter was written in June 1959. Subsequent queries as to a possible change of mind have elicited no reply.

Latin American affairs had become a waste land of the State Department and the Foreign Service. With a few notable exceptions, it was a refuge for the untrained, the superannuated, the politically deserving and the mediocre. It had probably been significantly infiltrated by pro-Communist elements during the years when the State Department Latin American affairs division was run by an alleged Soviet spy.

In the late 1950's, leftwing attitudes were still predominant. Appeasers of Communism, leftwing socialists and extreme New Dealers, united in their hatred of free enterprise and other basic American institutions, were strongly entrenched in this part of the Foreign Service.

Secretary of State John Foster Dulles regarded Latin America as safe from a cold war standpoint and hence of only secondary importance. In 1954, Dulles rammed a resolution through the 10th Inter-American Conference, meeting at Caracas, which stated that Communist "domination . . . of any American state" would be regarded as a threat to the security of the Hemisphere as a whole which should be answered by consultation and collective action. With this instrument for concerted Pan American action to suppress Red beachheads in the Americas, Dulles believed that the freedom of the Hemisphere from Soviet aggression had been secured. He had no way of anticipating that his own death would be followed by a period of indecisive leadership of American foreign policy in which this excellent instrument would remain unused. The period of Castro worship in the State Department dates from the time when Secretary Dulles was stricken with cancer and hence unable to enforce the indomitable anti-Communist policies to which he was personally dedicated on such weak or appeasement-minded subordinates as Undersecretary Herter and the ineffable Messrs. Rubottom and Wieland.

The State Department and Castro

Thus, mediocrity, the need to reward the politically faithful and the over-confidence of the Secretary of State had conspired to create a condition of affairs in which ultra "liberals" and leftwingers could gradually bend American policy toward Cuba in accordance with their ideological preconceptions.

"Cuba was handed to Castro and the Communists by a

combination of Americans in the same way that China was handed to the Communists," Senators James O. Eastland of Mississippi and Thomas J. Dodd of Connecticut concluded in a statement released to the press on September 11, 1960. Summarizing the testimony of former U.S. Ambassadors to Cuba Gardner and Smith, the two Senators stated:

"The testimony of both these gentlemen demonstrates that American foreign policy is not made in the office of Secretary Herter on the fifth floor of the State Department," said Eastland and Dodd. "It is made on the fourth floor, by the unknown policy planners and memo makers who fill the Secretary's 'in' basket." According to Messrs. Smith and Gardner, Fidel Castro was the hero of the In-Basket Brigade. They worked with pro-Castro elements in the American press to make Castro appear as Robin Hood. They misguided American opinion in exactly the same way the In-Basket Brigade of 1945 misguided American opinion with the myth that the Chinese Communists were 'agrarian reformers.'

"The State Department has not been cleansed of those elements whose policies contributed so much to the loss of China to the free world. Secretary Herter, the man on the quarter deck, is not in charge of the ship."

The Senators drew particular attention to this statement of Ambassador Smith.

"We helped to overthrow the Batista dictatorship which was pro-American, only to install the Castro dictatorship, which is pro-Russian."

According to former Ambassador Smith, the agencies of the United States Government which "had a hand in bringing pressure to overthrow the Batista government" were "certain influential people, influential sources in the State Department, lower down echelons in the CIA" and "representatives of the majority of the United States Government agencies which have anything to do with the Embassy" in Cuba.

Ambassador Smith made the remarkable disclosure that Wieland sent him to none other than Herbert Matthews to get his briefing on Cuban affairs before departing for his post at Havana. This took place in 1957 after Matthews had published his articles glorifying Castro. While the order came from Wieland, it must have been approved by Rubottom.

Wieland's biography in *Who's Who in America* reveals that his formal higher education consisted of one year at Villanova College, not an impressive qualification for a post of strategic importance in the Foreign Service. As a young man in Cuba, Wieland was associated with the terrorist ABC organization. In Cuba in the early 1930's, he became a friend of Undersecretary of State Sumner Welles. He entered the Foreign Service at a time when its Latin American division was under an alleged Soviet agent.

Pertinent testimony concerning Wieland reads:

Senator EASTLAND. Who were those individuals in the State Department?

Mr. SMITH. That were doing what, sir?

Senator EASTLAND. That were slanting the news that way; that were telling falsehoods; that were pro-Castro?

Mr. SMITH. There were quite a few, Senator.

Senator EASTLAND. Who were they?

Mr. SMITH. Do I have to mention names?

Senator EASTLAND. Yes. We have reasons, Mr. Smith . . .

Mr. SMITH. Yes. I believe Wieland, William Wieland, and that is as far as I would like to go in the State Department. I had my own troubles in the Embassy, but I corrected it in the Embassy by never allowing one single cable to go out that did not have my signature.

I wrote practically every political cable that went out.

The record suggests that Wieland, who exerted "a strong influence" on Rubottom, was probably the latter's protégé. His rapid rise in the Department dates from the calamitous appointment of Rubottom to a policy position in Latin American affairs.

Like Rubottom, Wieland was an eyewitness of the Bogotazo for he served in Colombia in a minor capacity during 1947-49 and receives brief mention in Ambassador Beaulac's memoirs. Like Rubottom, he was in a strategic position to know and remember the sinister role which Fidel Castro played there. Again like Rubottom, he never learned the facts or else learned them and forgot them or else neither forgot them nor chose to disclose them. He and Rubottom consistently turned deaf ears to the warnings given them by patriotic American diplomats that Castro's movement was Communist-dominated.

Ambassador Gardner had a brief contact with Wieland. The latter was in the American Embassy in Havana "for a very short time," Gardner testified. "I was very glad to see him go." Before that Wieland had served in Brazil, but U.S. Ambassador Pawling "got him out" because he thought that Wieland was "much too far on the left."

The case of William Arthur Wieland suggests that there is something fundamentally wrong with the American Foreign Service and that there is need for drastic remedies. Here was a man with practically no formal education, who was deemed undesirable because of leftism by two American Amabassadors according to the sworn testimony of one of them. By the time he was in his middle forties, his bureaucratic career had been, to put it mildly, undistinguished. Yet, under a Republican Administration and at a time when the United States was supposedly committed to a relentless global struggle against Communism, Wieland was the person chosen to represent the In-Basket Brigade for the Caribbean.

There were minor figures in the Foreign Service who played the Castro game to the detriment of the national interests of the United States. When ordered by Senator Eastland to identify the pro-Castro elements in the American Embassy in Havana, Ambassador Smith reluctantly named "the Chief of the Political Section, John Topping, and the Chief of the CIA Section. It was revealed that the No. 2 CIA man in the embassy had given unwarranted and undue encouragement to the revolutionaries. This came out in the trials of naval officers after the Cienfuegos revolution of September 1957."

What the No. 2 CIA man apparently did was to meet with pro-Castro officers in the Cuban Navy who were plotting mutiny and either assure them or leave them with the understanding that, if their revolt were successful, the United States "would recognize the revolutionaries." Mr. Smith had to call a meeting of the Embassy staff and lay down the law that neither the Ambassador nor anyone else in the Embassy could commit the United States "as to whom the United States would recognize; that there were only two people in the United States that had that authority: One was the Secretary of State and the other was the President of the United States." It is difficult to believe that any Government official could be stupid enough not to know that any discussion with mutineers and conspirators about U.S. diplomatic recognition was wholly impermissible.

Finally, we come back to Rubottom. The testimony of the two former Ambassadors casts somewhat fitful light on this enigmatic figure. Both tended to try to justify or palliate his conduct. Thus, Ambassador Smith said:

"In all due justice to Roy Rubottom, I think that Roy Rubottom was under terrific pressure from segments of the press, from certain Members of Congress, from the avalanche of Castro sympathizers and revolutionary sympathizers who daily descended upon the State Department, and Rubottom may have taken the line of least resistance."

It is probably true that he was under pressure. But a public servant is supposed to have the backbone to resist such pressure when the vital interests of his country are concerned.

Arthur Gardner implied that the trouble with Rubottom was not so much lack of moral courage as stupidity and incapacity. He testified:

"And then he came to Washington, and was assistant—or I don't know what particular rank he had—in the Latin American Department. Why they put him in, I will never know. In the first place, he was in the process of learning Spanish. In the second place, I felt he had absolutely no background of experience."

Rubottom had gone to a Texas Methodist college. From 1943 on, he had held diplomatic jobs in Latin America or concerning Latin America. He was named Assistant Secretary of State for Latin American affairs in 1957. Thus, if Ambassador Gardner is correct, he had been working in the Hispanic and Hispanic American field for 14 years, but hadn't bothered to learn the language! Can one imagine a Soviet official responsible for an area as incompetent or ill-trained as that?

The alleged ignorance and incapacity of Rubottom did not prevent his playing a major role in furthering a policy adverse to American interests. Ambassador Gardner tried desperately to alert the responsible leaders of the State Department to the fact that "Castro talked and acted like a Communist, and should not be supported by the United States." He approached then Undersecretary Christian Herter and such top men as Loy Henderson and Robert Murphy, but he got nowhere. If these men turned deaf ears to him, they can be partially exculpated on the grounds that Latin America was not their field and they were "badly advised."

Ambassador Gardner also tried to persuade Rubottom, but got nowhere. The testimony reads:

Mr. GARDNER. Well, I talked to Loy Henderson.

Senator DODD. Mr. Rubottom?

Mr. GARDNER. Yes, I talked to Rubottom. But he was not at all interested.

Senator DODD. You mean by that he was not interested in your views in the situation?

Mr. GARDNER. Yes. He is a nice chap, and means well, and I have nothing but high regard for him personally, but I think he was entirely off on the wrong track, and it has been proved. Without putting it down, let me just explain what I mean.

(Discussion off the record.)

Senator Dodd. Did you discuss this situation—by this situation I mean the Castro-Batista situation, with Robert Murphy?

Mr. Gardner. Yes.

Senator Dodd. And what did you find his reaction to be?

Mr. Gardner. I found he was so badly advised. We had a pleasant talk, but got nowhere. He had an idea that Batista was a gorilla.

Senator Dodd. Did he think favorably of Castro?

Mr. Gardner. No. But he felt so strongly against Batista, that anybody would have been better, I imagine, is the way he would put it.

Senator Dodd. I see. During these conversations with these several persons whom you have named, did you, from time to time, tell any one of them, or all of them, that Castro talked and acted like a Communist, and should not be supported by the United States?

Mr. Gardner. Yes. But the purpose of these conversations always seemed to be was whether Castro carried a Communist card or not. We all knew—I think everybody knew—that his brother, Raul, was a Communist. But they seemed to argue about it as if that was important.

Senator Dodd. You mean the technicality of party membership was made a matter of importance rather than his general attitude?

Mr. Gardner. Yes, that is right.

Senator Dodd. I understand.

Mr. Gardner, can you tell us again specifically, if you remember, did you say this to Mr. Murphy, and to Mr. Rubottom, and to Mr. Herter, or to anyone else?

Mr. Gardner. No, I didn't say it to Herter.

Senator Dodd. Did you say it to Rubottom?

Mr. Gardner. In a nice way—yes, I said it to Rubottom. And I talked to Loy about it. And Murphy, I did talk to him about it. I don't remember the conversation, but that was my reason for going to see him.

Senator Dodd. But you generally did discuss this matter?

Mr. Gardner. Yes, that is right.

Senator Dodd. And you gave him this warning?

Mr. Gardner. That is right.

Senator Dodd. And you felt, I take it, from your testimony, that you got no interest, no encouragement?

Mr. Gardner. No.

Summarizing the sorry and disillusioning consequences of his effort to serve his country in Cuba, Ambassador Gardner said that on his return to America he had been "ignored, overlooked and circumvented" by the State Department.

Ambassador Smith had somewhat similar experiences. He reached the conclusion that policy determination by the middle echelon clique of pseudo-liberals and semi-competents on the fourth floor of Foggy Bottom, by the so-called In-Basket Brigade, had been fatal to the interests of the United States. He testified:

"I believe that the policies are determined in the lower echelon, and by the time the higher echelon receives them, policies have already been made, and they have to live by them.

"I would like to recommend that some higher authority, such as the National Security Council of the United States, determine what our attitude toward another nation should be. Then all the actions of the State Department should be guided according to such policy as laid down by the National Security Council. I am sure the decision of the National Security Council would be arrived at from what is in the best interest of the United States.

"If they believed it was in the best interest of the United States to be friendly to another power and to give aid to that power, then our actions along that line should be guided accordingly."

In discussing the actions of the rather undistinguished

group of officials who cast American policy toward Cuba in the suicidal shape that it was to assume, no accusation of lack of patriotism has been made or is intended. To an undetermined extent, the basic problem was stupidity and incompetence. It should, however, be added that stupidity is at present an incurable disease since, with all its miracle drugs, modern medicine has not discovered how to inject brains into empty skulls. A nation challenged and globally on the defensive as ours is today can afford neither second-raters nor incompetents in high places.

One of the first straws, showing the changing direction of the winds, was that the State Department instructed Earl E. T. Smith, the new Ambassador to Cuba, to go to none other than Herbert L. Matthews for briefing. Fortunately, Smith was not the sort of man who would be swayed by the pro-Castro zealot of the *New York Times*. When Ambassador Smith reached Havana, he proceeded to pursue a realistic policy that corresponded with both American and Cuban national interests. At the time, Castro did not as yet have any impressive military force although he was being built up by Matthews and other partisan correspondents. The Cuban situation had not yet polarized to a choice between Batista corruption and Castro totalitarianism.

Ambassador Smith urged Batista to step down in favor of a junta of outstanding military and civilian leaders who would govern only long enough to guarantee free elections. The Cuban strong man was irritated by this proposal that he withdraw before completing his constitutional term.[2] He did, however, promise Ambassador Smith that Cuba would have fair and free elections when his own term expired. This promise did not seem out of character since Batista had done precisely this in 1944.

[2] A similar proposal was made to Batista by Manuel Cardinal Arteaga, Archbishop of Havana, in early 1958. The Catholic dignitary called for a "national union government" to end civil strife and bloodshed and restore "normal political life." Batista refused with visible annoyance. v. Phillips, *op. cit.*, p. 348.

The fate of Cuba now depended on these promised forth-coming presidential elections. Meanwhile, the winds were shifting further to the left in Washington. In January 1958, Ambassador Smith came back to the United States for consultation. At the request of the State Department, he held a press conference at Foggy Bottom.

Smith was asked off the record whether the United States could do business with Castro. His reply was that it could not.[3]

In response to a further question, Smith explained that the United States could deal only with a government which would maintain law and order, honor its international obligations and have the support of its people. The Ambassador added that, in his opinion, it was questionable whether Castro could maintain law and order or would honor Cuba's international obligations.

Twenty-four hours after these off-the-record statements had been made, they had leaked and both Castro in the mountains and Representative Porter in Washington knew about them. It was also reported that Ambassador Smith had called Castro a Communist. That was untrue. He had merely said that Castro's movement was infiltrated by Communists and that the extent of that infiltration was unknown.

This press conference made Smith the target of various "liberals" in Congress and the State Department and of the American foreign correspondents who were engaged in disseminating Castro propaganda. He was branded as an enemy of the 26th of July Movement and as hostile toward the truly progressive forces of Cuba. As had been the case with Ambassador Gardner, a smear campaign was waged against Ambassador Smith which undermined his influence both in Havana and in Washington.

[3] I have been authorized to report these off-the-record questions and answers.

The Castro Propaganda Machine

To arouse passionate interest in the Castro cause, to transform it from just another Latin American uprising into a crusade for freedom, it was necessary that it be presented to the world in romantic and idealistic terms. The propaganda task was to combine accurate reporting on ideologically neutral matters with the sort of naive enthusiasm characteristic of religious revivals. Another task—one that seemed *prima facie* impossible because of the avalanche of evidence—was to persuade the American public that the Communist Party of Cuba was supporting, not Fidel Castro, but Batista! Finally, as the dictatorship began to weaken, the key propaganda requirement was to drive home the dogma that the only realistic choice was between Fidel Castro and Batista.

These tasks were accomplished brilliantly. Some of the American reporters who played this game were childish in political matters, adolescently romantic about politics or else inherently rebellious and resentful of the established order. These people generally deceived themselves before deluding others.

Of the propagandists, Fidel Castro himself was one of the most astute. He issued bloodthirsty pronouncements in Cuba to spread terror among the neutral population of the island, but he turned a benign and liberal face to United States correspondents. Thus, in May 1958, Castro gave a written interview to Jules Dubois in which, according to the latter, he made the following statements:

"I have never been nor am I a Communist . . . Never has the 26th of July Movement talked about socializing or nationalizing the industries. This is simply stupid fear of our revolution.

"We have proclaimed from the first day that we fight for the full enforcement of the Constitution of 1940 . . . Comprised therein is free enterprise and invested capital as well as many other economic, civic and political rights . . . The dictatorship must be replaced by a provisional government of entirely civilian character that will return the country to normality and hold general elections within a period of no more than a year . . .

"Personally, I do not aspire to any post and I consider that there is sufficient proof that I fight for the good of my people, without any personal or egotistical ambition soiling my conduct." [4]

The Role of Herbert Matthews

If there was any single American who could be held responsible for the Cuban tragedy, it was Herbert L. Matthews of the *New York Times*. A veteran foreign correspondent in his late fifties, Matthews was a man who had always preferred choosing sides to dispassionate reporting. At first, there were no indications of Communist sympathies. In the Far Eastern crisis, which he reported in the late 1920's, Matthews was pro-Japanese because he liked the "charm and hospitality" of the island people. When Mussolini invaded Ethiopia in 1935, Matthews became an enthusiast for the Italians. Later, he reminisced: "If you start from the premise that a lot of rascals are having a fight, it is not unnatural to want to see the victory of the rascal you like, and I liked the Italians during that scrimmage more than I did the British or the Abyssinians."

The Spanish Civil War was a turning point. Matthews "was outspokenly partisan for the Communist-backed Loyalist forces" [5] and would later be branded as a Red by the Spanish Government. He was rebuked by Arthur Sulzberger, the publisher of the *New York Times* for having painted Loyalist prospects in rosy colors at a time when

---

[4] Dubois, *op. cit.*, pp. 261-5.
[5] "The *Times* & Cuba," *Time*, July 27, 1959, pp. 47-8.

defeat was looming. This charge didn't bother reporter Matthews. He wrote in his memoirs:

"Even then, heartsick and discouraged as I was, something sang inside of me. I, like the Spaniards, had fought my war and lost, but I couldn't be persuaded that I had set too bad an example." [6]

Any reporter has a duty to his paper and to the public to write the facts as objectively as possible. He cannot serve as a psychological warfare officer. The latter is part of an army. His duty is to work for victory and he owes no duty to those he deceives. The foreign correspondent who engages surreptitiously in psychological warfare, however, is in an entirely different position. If he twists the news for partisan purposes, he breaks faith with those who employ him and with the reading public which assumes his honesty.

The psychological warfare agent, whether overt or covert, professional or amateur, habitually seeks to exaggerate the strength and inflate the prospects of his side. This is essentially a counterintelligence operation, designed to feed false data to the enemy G-2. When an American correspondent takes sides in a foreign civil war, a proper question is whether his dispatches are designed to inform his own countrymen or to misinform that foreign faction or government which he considers he is fighting.

Castro "has strong ideas of liberty, democracy, social justice, the need to restore the constitution, to hold elections," Matthews wrote in 1957. Two years later, Castro in power proved by his conduct that all of these statements were false. Most of the American reporters he had deceived tried to forget the Cuban nightmare and wrote about other things. Jules Dubois and Ruby Hart Phillips recognized the mistakes they had made and, in sound and penetrating dispatches, exposed the Communist subversion of Cuba. The free trade unions of the Americas turned against Castro. Non-Communist leftwing leaders, such as Figueras in Costa

[6] *The Education of a Correspondent,* quoted in *Time, op. cit.*

Rica, Muñoz Marin in Puerto Rico and Betancourt in Venezuela, either terminated their alliance with him or attacked
him.

In short, Fidel Castro's support was rapidly narrowing to
the international Communist movement and inveterate followers of Soviet causes. Herbert L. Matthews remained
among the faithful. Proceeding to Cuba in July 1959, Matthews discovered that nothing had changed. "This is not a
Communist revolution in any sense of the word," he
revealed, "and there are no Communists in positions of control." He saw no reason to be disenchanted with Castro's
revolution. Matthews would go so far as to concede that the
regime might have made mistakes. His explanation was:
"Youth must sow its wild oats."

William Morgan, Freedom Fighter

Now we return to a specific point in time—1958. Under
the combined pressure of Soviet arms and gold and American propaganda, the Batista regime was beginning to crum-
ble. At this juncture, Fidel Castro's basic propaganda task
was to convince world opinion that his movement was the
only possible way out for Cuba. Accordingly, the bona fide
liberal opposition to Batista was smeared. Its leaders were
portrayed as corruptionists and cowards because they refused to join Fidel Castro and his Communists in the mountains. One American correspondent, Ray Brennan, found it
almost impossible to mention ex-President Prío Socarrás
without adding the characterization "chicken fancier." Of
course, there is nothing disgraceful about running a poultry
farm, but the word "chicken" just happens to have another
and very different connotation in American speech.

Nobody who knew anything about American public opinion would imagine that it would accept Fidel Castro as a
modern folk hero without some very definite assurances that
Castro was not only not a Communist, but actively engaged

in fighting Communism. Herbert L. Matthews gave the public assurance on both points. Perhaps this wasn't quite good enough and an additional witness might help.

In any event, in 1958, the ubiquitous Matthews returned to the Sierra Maestra where he dredged up a new hero, William Alexander Morgan, American volunteer fighting in the ranks of Castro's forces. Matthews quoted, or purportedly quoted, Morgan at length on the latter's wise and idealistic political philosophy.

"Over the years, we as Americans have found that dictators and Communists are bad people with whom to do business," Matthews quoted Morgan as declaring. "Yet here is a dictator (Batista) who has been supported by the Communists and he would fall from power tomorrow if it were not for American aid."

There was a photograph of Morgan among his fellow Cuban guerrilleros who, of course, allegedly had great admiration for him. Herbert Matthews presented his newest hero to the American reading public as "married and with two children, a veteran of the U. S. Army in World War II . . . adept at judo . . . ," in short, quite a man.

The build-up on Morgan was slightly inaccurate. Morgan had deserted his wife and children. He never served in World War II nor did anything to defend his country. He was neither a paratrooper nor a specialist in judo, but an infantry private in the U. S. Army of occupation in Japan.

The real Morgan was an undereducated delinquent and military criminal. In November 1947, he was placed in confinement in Kyoto, Japan, whereupon he overpowered his guard, stole the latter's .45 caliber pistol and uniform and escaped.

When he was apprehended, he was found guilty both of escape and armed robbery. The fact that he had a prior conviction under military law was taken into consideration and he was sentenced:

"To be dishonorably discharged from the service, to forfeit all pay and allowance due or to become due, and to be confined at hard labor, at such place as the reviewing authority may direct, for five (5) years."[7]

The heroic freedom fighter of the Matthews dispatch turned out to have spent much of his military career in Chillicothe Federal Reformatory. Here he was placed in solitary on several occasions for fighting, attempted escape, refusal to work and attempted arson. Like Fidel Castro, though on a lesser scale, Morgan was a superannuated juvenile delinquent, addicted to crimes of violence and to betrayal. His military record was dishonorable. A foreign correspondent, concerned with finding the facts and reporting them dispassionately to his countrymen, might have been expected to check the publicly available records of the Adjutant General's Office of the Army before palming off "paratrooper" Morgan as an all-American hero.

The Communist Party and Batista

Meanwhile, the legend that the Cuban Communist Party backed Batista was assiduously spread. The truth of the matter was that the Party had suffered horribly under the Batista repression; some of its best cadres had been killed, manhandled or imprisoned, and the Party was cowed and badly demoralized.

A much more important consideration was that Castro had been advised to have nothing to do with known Cuban Communists or with the Party by the directors of *Rambla, Estancia, A.T.* and other Soviet apparatuses. The Soviet view was that it was vital that the Castro movement be without visible Communist taint and hence eligible for world-wide liberal support. When specific Communist cadres were needed, these could be supplied by the Soviet apparatuses. In those instances where a specific member of the Cuban

[7] Headquarters 25th Infantry Division, APO 25 (Osaka, Japan), General Court Martial Orders No. 8.

Communist Party was needed, he could be withdrawn from the Party, incorporated into one of the Soviet nets and used by the Castro movement while under its discipline.[8]

The Communist Party as an organization, though not all of its leaders, was kept in ignorance of the existence, scope and operations of the Soviet nets. The latter apparently took no action to prevent the decimation of the open Communist Party by Batista's repressive agencies since this served both to create martyrs and to deflect attention from the underground.[9] If the procedures used by the Comintern in Germany under Hitler were followed in Cuba, it is safe to assume that members of the Soviet apparatuses who had infiltrated BRAC and SIM arrested unreliable or expendable open Communists, thus demonstrating their efficiency and their loyalty to the Batista regime. Double agents, working in counterespionage agencies, have the habit of climbing to power on the skulls and corpses of their comrades.

Castro already had the active support of the underground nets; he had no need of the open Communist Party; in fact, it would have been a dead albatross around his neck. A semi-underground Communist youth group, using the cover name, *Flechas* (Arrows), recruited combat teams and sent them to the Sierra Maestra to join Castro. As Domingo tells the story, Fidel had been thoroughly briefed about the danger, from a public relations standpoint, of admitting this group. The first batch was turned down on grounds of physical unfitness. When a second group of nine youths was sent, the three girls were accepted, but not the men, the reason being that there was a good deal of grumbling about the fact that in the Sierra Maestra the leaders had women, but not the rank and file. After this humiliation, *Flechas* gave up trying to send people to Castro.[10]

Actually, these conspirative precautions were not nearly

[8] Domingo, *op. cit.*
[9] *Ibid.*
[10] *Ibid.*

as comprehensive or as effectively applied as this schematism suggests. We have seen that Carlos Rafael Rodriguez, who was not only a member of the Political Bureau of the Cuban Communist Party, but its brains, went to the Sierra Maestra to bring Fidel Castro almost a million dollars.

According to a report from the Cuban underground on the background of the arrest and imprisonment of Fidel Castro's close colleague, Major Hubert Matos:

"As early as 1957, Matos was ordered to facilitate the passage of known Communist activists. On direct orders of Fidel Castro, he arranged entry into the mountains for a stream of such ranking Reds as Ladislas Carvajal, Fidel Domenech, Captain Rafael Avalo, Captain Francisco Manchon and many others.

By 1957, the *Intelligence Digest* was able to publish detailed reports about the Communist affiliations of leaders of the Castro movement. This information was well known to BRAC. It was published on two occasions and sent to a key list of several hundred United States Government officials concerned with Latin American affairs by Colonel John Kiefer, a veteran officer of the Yardley "Black Chamber," probably the finest counterintelligence organization for its size the United States ever had. Kiefer at the time was both a Deputy Director of BRAC and a registered foreign agent for the Batista government. The Kiefer reports may have been discounted as propaganda,[11] but the same reason could not have been advanced for discounting the similar findings of United States agencies.

The "secret" of the Communist cloven hoof of the 26th of July Movement was well-kept because people in power in Washington did not want to believe in it. Among the reasons

---

[11] American Government officials have become very sophisticated about such matters, so much so that they seldom bother to read anything which has the open imprint of a foreign dictatorship on its face. Hence, one enterprising U. S. intelligence officer arranged to have the Kiefer reports airmailed to him from Washington to Havana, whereupon he paraphrased them and airmailed them back to Washington as his own findings.

for this was the then fashionable crusade against Latin American dictatorships and a reaction against McCarthyism, which had reached such a point that some officials wanted to see a man's Party book before concluding that he was a Communist.

There was some scintilla of evidence that the Communists were also playing the Batista side of the street. Acute American correspondents noted that, despite Batista's war to the death against Communism, there were plenty of Communists in leading positions in the trade union movement. The explanation of this fact was that Batista was by no means an absolute dictator and the trade union federation (CTC) remained independent. For the decade prior to Castro's seizure of power, the CTC was run by Eusebio Mujal, a charter member of the Cuban Communist Party and member of its Central Committee. Mujal broke with the Party and from at least the 1940's on was one of its most bitter and implacable enemies.

Mujal believed, however, that Communism must be fought in the trade unions by debate and on ideological grounds. He made an arrangement with Batista by which the suppressive agencies of the government left those Communists alone who managed to get elected to trade union posts. Throughout the second Batista era, from about 5% to 15% of the trade union delegates were Communists. Mujal and his Autenticos fought them in the unions and, in their opinion, by means of this fight strengthened the anti-Communist convictions of the Cuban labor movement as a whole. (Whether or not this appraisal is correct may some day be tested by the role of the labor unions in a future struggle against Soviet domination in Cuba.)

Early in 1958, the Cuban Communist Party played the gambit of threatening to back Fidel Castro unless Batista stopped arresting Reds. The Cuban *caudillo* foolishly caved in and a more intensive Communist infiltration of the trade unions and the Government followed.

The open Party was in no hurry to announce its support of Castro. The result in terms of United States policy would surely be unfavorable to the 26th of July Movement. Powerful Communist contingents were already entrenched in the Castro leadership. The uncommitted position of the Party enabled it to build its fences in the trade unions and the bureaucracy.

As early as January 1958, one of the top Communist leaders in the Cuban labor movement told Dr. Marquez Sterling that the Party would throw its support to Fidel Castro.[12] The open decision to do this was delayed until the United States Government had pulled the rug out from under Batista by imposing an arms embargo.

The Party had no desire to sacrifice its cadres needlessly. When Castro proclaimed a general strike for April 9, 1958, the tenth anniversary of the Bogotázo, the Communist unions did not support it. "You don't see Communists rushing out in the streets to get killed," was the comment one Red made to New York Times correspondent Ruby Hart Phillips.

When Castro took power, the Cuban Communist Party spoke openly of the support it had given his movement. "We the Cuban Communists have done our part in the Cuban revolution to overthrow the bloody tyranny of Batista which served as the instrument of imperialistic interests and was supported by imperialism," Politburo member Carlos Rafael Rodriguez boasted in April 1959.[13] A 1959 pamphlet of the American Communist Party wrote of the "strong contingent of party members and sympathizers (which) belonged to the rebel forces" and the "mass actions" in support of Castro organized by the Cuban C.P.[14]

[12] Name withheld at the request of Dr. Marquez Sterling. The Communist leader in question is in Cuba and might get in trouble if it were revealed that he had discussed Party plans with a "counterrevolutionary."
[13] "Fear of Reds' Role in Castro Regime Alarming Havana" by R. Hart Phillips, New York Times, Havana, April 22, 1959.
[14] Communist Party of the United States of America, The Cuban Revolution and the Tasks of the Communist Party, U. S. A., 1959.

On February 1, 1959, *Pravda* declared that, from the very inception of Castro's struggle, "our party considered it its first duty to aid the rebels, giving them the correct orientation and the support of the popular masses. The party headed the battle of the peasants for land and thereby increased its authority among the peasantry.

"Our party . . . appealed to the popular masses to support Fidel Castro in every way . . ."

The best one could say about the theory that the Cuban Communist Party supported Batista, rather than Castro, is that there were enough complicating elements in the politics of the situation to make it possible for a foreign correspondent who was either ignorant of Communism or not particularly diligent to fall into that erroneous interpretation honestly.[15]

The Presidential Elections

In the spring of 1958, a realistic United States policy toward Cuba was still possible. Batista had proclaimed presidential elections for June 1, 1958. His hand-picked successor was opposed by Dr. Grau San Martin for the Autentico Party and Dr. Carlos Marquez Sterling for the Orthodox Party. These opposition candidates were both supporters of democracy and enemies of Communism.

The United States Government could, at this juncture,

[15] The factor of naïveté and failure to investigate the facts should never be ignored in considering the garbled way in which the Cuban story was reported. For example, when Castro fired President Manuel Urrutia Lleo, a liberal, in the summer of 1959 and replaced him by Dr. Oswaldo Dorticos, the U. S. press as a whole took the line that the new man was a leftist, but not a Communist. The readily ascertainable facts were that Dorticos had been a candidate for public office on the Communist ticket in his native Pinar del Rio, that he had been the secretary to Juan Marinello, President of the Cuban Communist Party, for over a decade and that, in that capacity, he had regularly collected the salary checks of the Communist Senators and Deputies, during the years when the Party was legal, turning the checks over to the Party and paying the Red legislators the so-called "party maximum" salary. Does the Cuban climate make reporters lazy or does it merely attract lazy reporters?

have released the voluminous information in its files, showing that the Fidel Castro movement was Communist-infiltrated and Communist-controlled. It could have made it
clear that the United States would consider the victory of
the Castro movement a threat to its security. The State Department could have made it plain that this country desired
Cuba to return to democracy, eliminating both Batista and
his chosen successor. It could have added that arms and
materiel in sufficient quantity to crush the Castro insurrection would be made available provided Batista actually conducted free elections.

The entrenched position of the pro-Castro forces in the
U. S. Government and the pernicious effect of the pro-Castro
propaganda of American publicists made it politically impossible to take a position as clear-cut and decisive as this.
Instead of warning about Communist infiltration of the Castro movement, the State Department blandly whitewashed
the insurgents of any Red taint.

Ambassador Smith wanted free elections in Cuba. His view
was that the United States could quietly support Marquez
Sterling, who was a Professor of Economics at Havana University and who had played a major role in drafting the
advanced labor and social legislation embodied in the 1940
Cuban Constitution. The American Embassy understood
that Marquez Sterling, if elected, would serve a short term
as President, that is to say that he would use his tenure in
office to negotiate an end to the civil war and to have new
elections held once law and order were re-established.

This program required a firm understanding with both
sides that they would cooperate in ensuring fair elections.
Batista promised Ambassador Smith that he would do this.
However, Castro worked energetically to prevent the elections from being held. His position was that there was no
possible middle ground of compromise between his movement and the dictatorship. The old politicians were discredited; they did not represent Cuba. This line was entirely

logical in terms of the Communist program of sweeping away, not merely the dictatorship, but the institutions of Cuban representative government as well.

It is worth pointing out that, despite the efforts of the left-wing clique to smear former American Ambassador Arthur Gardner as a Batista stooge, the fact of the matter was that he pursued the same realistic and constructive policy as his successor.

"We could have prevented it all and we didn't," Gardner said in his *Standard-Times* interview. "If we'd carried out normal relations with Batista, just carried out our contracts, he would have got out as scheduled, come to live in Florida, and been replaced by an ideal candidate."

"A pro-Batista man?" Gardner was asked.

"No. Marquez Sterling, a doctor, whom everybody loved, was Batista's opponent. Ironically, although against Batista, he had to flee Cuba because of Castro."

Marquez Sterling Negotiates

Marquez Sterling sent a young emissary, named Cosio, to the Sierra Maestra with a message urging Castro to rescind his order boycotting the elections. Marquez said the opposition parties needed guaranties from Batista, but they needed guaranties from Castro as well.

Castro replied in a letter, stating that the revolution would win before the elections could be held. Previously, he had sent an emissary to Marquez Sterling offering him the Presidency of Cuba provided he would come out in support of the 26th of July Movement. On that occasion, Marquez Sterling had replied that he wanted to be President, but by constitutional means. He would run for President in the elections and would support Castro's insurrectionary movement if, and only if, Batista refused to permit a free and fair choice by the voters.

There had been other contacts between Marquez Sterling

and Castro supporters. In late March of 1958, Herbert L. Matthews appeared at Marquez Sterling's house. Matthews reminded his host that his ancestors had played a distinguished role in all of Cuba's independence struggles. Marquez Sterling replied that his family background had nothing to do with the Castro issue. The reason he was not supporting Castro was that the movement was Communist-dominated and he didn't want to see a Communist Cuba.

At this point, Matthews showed Marquez Sterling the 22-point manifesto of Fidel Castro, issued from the Sierra Maestra, as proof of the insurrectionary leader's freedom from any Red taint. This document made a most unfavorable impression on Marquez Sterling. It seemed to make any peaceful solution of the Cuban problem impossible.

Promulgated on March 17, 1958, the manifesto was a declaration of total war against the Batista regime to be waged by military operations, terror and general strike. "In order to give the leaders of the revolutionary movement time to act, the campaign of extermination against all those who serve the tyranny under arms will not begin before April 5. From that date, the war will be relentlessly waged . . . The people will have to annihilate the military wherever they are found as the worst enemies of freedom and happiness." Anyone serving in an office of trust in the executive branch of the government after April 5 was to be "considered guilty of treason." Moreover, "any citizen enlisting in the armed forces subsequent to the date hereof will be subject to court-martial and be judged as a criminal." [16]

This bloodthirsty pronouncement showed that Castro was determined to prevent elections at all costs. Six days later, President Batista announced that elections would be postponed from June 1st to November 3rd.

Marquez Sterling sent his emissary back to the Sierra Maestra in a last effort to get Castro to support orderly constitutional processes. Castro replied by promulgating

[16] Translated by Dubois, *op. cit.*, pp. 237-40.

Law #2 of the Sierra Maestra. This demanded that all candidates in the elections withdraw at once. In the rural areas, those who failed to do so would suffer "from ten years imprisonment to the death sentence." In the cities, "the death sentence may be executed against the guilty either by the rebel troops or by the militia which operate in the urban zones."

The pretext for this barbarous order was that the opposition candidates were guilty of "betrayal of the interests of the Fatherland and the revolution" in furtherance of "their bastard personal conveniences." They were branded as stooges of Batista, men in his pay, window dressing for the dictatorship. Even such a competent reporter as Jules Dubois would repeat this charge in his laudatory biography of Fidel Castro. The simplest proof that it was a lie is that Castro, after having been in full possession of the archives of the Batista government for over a year and a half, has produced no evidence substantiating it.

Law #2 of the Sierra Maestra gave every Fidelista a hunting license to murder the candidates of liberal parties who were trying to fight Batista by legal means. Many candidates were intimidated and withdrew. Despite two attempts on his life by Castro agents, Dr. Marquez Sterling did not. The elections were held, but Batista broke his pledge to Ambassador Smith and rigged them. By that time, it was too late for the outcome to make any difference.

As it became clear that the Castro movement had the support of the United States Government and was winning, more commentators followed the trail which Herbert Matthews had blazed. Edward R. Murrow of CBS staged a laudatory TV network program on the Castro movement. The normally hard-headed Ed Sullivan went into the Sierra Maestra for a television interview with its hairy armed prophet. Sullivan's technique was to ask leading questions such as: "You are not a Communist, are you, Fidel? You are a devout Catholic, aren't you?"—leaving Castro practically no time to answer.[17] The effect was comic in terms of theatre; tragic in terms of politics.

Thus, Castro floated to power on an ocean of Communist money and American misconceptions. He was described as pure by Assistant Secretary of State Roy Rubottom despite the fact that his record of Red associations and virulent hatred of the United States spanned more than a dozen years and was abundantly documented.

"American intelligence learned that the 26th of July people planned to kidnap and hold for ransom (such as recognition of Castro) all top officers of the United States in Cuba including the American Ambassador. They planned to hold their victims on the top floor of the chancellery right on the Malacon. "And then," Ambassador Gardner recalled, "if attention wasn't paid to this, they were going to drop one man after the other from the balcony." Accordingly, a Marine slept next to the Ambassador every night; he was followed on the streets at all times by a car with four guards with submachine guns; at night, listening devices in his bedroom broadcast and amplified his breathing to armed men standing guard in the corridors."

The failure of the middle-echelon policy-makers to react to this and similar insults to the United States was characteristic. In 1958, Raul Castro kidnaped 30 U.S. marines and sailors, 17 other American citizens and three Canadians. The State Department reaction was, not to compel the criminals to release the Americans, but to refuse to supply Batista with training planes to which he was entitled and for which he had paid. The reason given was fear of retaliation against the kidnaped persons.

American diplomats who formulate and execute policies of this sort might well have calling cards with the legend 'Have tails, will grovel.'

---

[17] It can be assumed that Fidel was gagged, not for any sinister reason, but simply because Sullivan discovered he was incapable of replying to any question with a short answer.

The classical adage is that the Gods make mad those whom they wish to destroy. In the case of the United States vis-à-vis Cuba, it would seem that the disease was not madness, but folly—and possibly something a great deal worse.

12

Economics of the Revolution

"There are no Communists
in positions of control in
Cuba."
—Herbert L. Matthews[1]

ONE of the many myths that the Castro regime would disseminate was that Cuba under its previous Presidents had been a land of oppressive poverty in which the common man had practically nothing. This is remote from the truth.

In 1957, according to estimates prepared for me in the International Monetary Fund, Cuba ranked fourth among the 20 Latin American Republics in per capita income. The average Cuban had an income in 1957 of $361 annually. This compared with $409 annually for Argentina, $281 for Brazil, $234 for Mexico and $88 for Paraguay. The average for Latin America as a whole was $284. The 1957 per capita income of Cuba was about one-sixth that of the United States, 90% that of Italy, significantly higher than that of Japan and six times that of India. All of these estimates are in dollars of 1957 purchasing power.[2]

[1] As reported in the *Washington Post*, April 22, 1960.
[2] The actual figures compiled in the International Monetary Fund are: United States $2,097, United Kingdom $946, Italy $404, Japan $252 and India $61.

Thus, in relationship both to the world as a whole and the Latin American region, the position of Cuba was rather favorable. The Economic and Technical Mission of the International Bank for Reconstruction and Development stated in its *Report on Cuba, 1951:*

"The general impression of members of the Mission, from observations and travels all over Cuba, is that living levels of the farmers, agricultural laborers, industrial workers, storekeepers, and others are higher all along the line than for corresponding groups in other tropical countries and in nearly all other Latin American countries. This does not mean that there is no dire poverty in Cuba, but simply that in comparative terms Cubans are better off, on the average, than people of these other areas."

In a 1956 report on Cuba, the Department of Commerce concluded: "Cuban national income has reached levels which give the Cuban people one of the highest standards of living in Latin America." [3]

Until Castro brought civil war to the island, there was encouraging economic growth. Between 1950 and mid-1958, Cuban national income rose from $1,623,000,000 to an estimated $2,170,000,000. When this is deflated by a 10% increase in living costs, the gain in national income during the period works out to about 22%.

During the entire period, there was a progressive increase in the share of national income going to labor. "Compensation of employees represented from 56 percent to 61 percent of total national income between 1946 and 1949, and from 59 to 65 percent between 1950 and 1954," the U. S. Department of Commerce reported in 1956.[4] The upward trend in wages continued and, in mid-1958, the Commerce Department noted: "Pay increases ranging from 10 percent to 30

[3] U. S. Department of Commerce, *Investment in Cuba,* Government Printing Office, Washington, D. C., 1956, p. 184.
[4] *Ibid,* p. 184.

percent were mainly obtained through collective bargaining and Government resolution." [5]

The island was becoming urbanized as a result of heavy investment in construction, industry and tourism, both domestic and foreign. By the 1950's, the typical Cuban was a town-dweller, not a plantation hand. In 1952, only 41.5% of the Cuban labor force was agricultural. In 1953, 34.9% of the population of the island lived in cities with 100,000 or more inhabitants; 43.4% lived in towns of from 5,000 to 100,000 inhabitants, and only 21.7% lived in places with fewer than 5,000 inhabitants.[6]

There were negative aspects to the picture. Almost a fourth of the Cuban population over the age of 10 was illiterate in 1953 and only 11.0% of the population had had more than 6 years of schooling.[7] The lack of education of the masses, particularly in the rural regions, meant that millions of Cubans could easily fall prey to ignorant or unscrupulous demagogues such as Castro and his associates. Moreover, the professional classes in Cuba were concentrated disproportionately in teaching and the law, with comparatively few engineers. A very large part of the highly educated element, in other words, was engaged in politics or political indoctrination and depended for its livelihood on the state.

At the turn of the century, Cuba suffered from "recurrent and devastating plagues, but today yellow fever and typhus have been eliminated, smallpox has been virtually stamped out, and typhoid and malaria have been brought under control," the Commerce Department wrote in 1956.[8] Two years later, it reported: "Cuba enjoys a high level of public health,

[5] U. S. Department of Commerce, *Economic Developments in Cuba 1958*, p. 1.
[6] Cuban census data reported in *Investment in Cuba*, pp. 178, 182.
[7] *Ibid*, p. 181. The last figure overstates the lack of formal education since the population enumerated consists of all persons 6 years old and over. Obviously the 6-to-12-year-olds could not be expected to have more than 6 years of schooling.
[8] *Investment in Cuba*, p. 180.

and general sanitation in Havana is good." [9] By 1958, malaria had been practically eliminated.

The last of the Castro myths to be exploded is that Cuban labor was downtrodden and oppressed and that Cuban trade unions were crushed under the iron heel of the Batista dictatorship. Writing in 1954, Ernst Schwarz, the Executive Secretary of the Committee on Latin American Affairs of the CIO, noted with satisfaction that the Cuban unions had eliminated Communist leadership in 1947. Schwarz added:

"The Cuban Confederation (of Labor) has successfully weathered the latest political storm caused by the Batista coup in March 1952. It has been able so to preserve its unity and strength as a powerful Cuban institution that even the new dictatorial regime has not dared to touch or eliminate it. The CTC[10] has enabled the Cuban workers to set an example to others of what can be achieved by labor unity and strength. Wages are far above those paid in many other parts of the Caribbean or, for that matter, Latin America. In addition, the eight-hour working day forms the basis for every one of the collective contracts concluded by the CTC's affiliated organizations. Modern types of social protection and insurance are provided in laws, public statutes, or union contracts; while funds maintained and administered in common by labor, employers, and the authorities provide adequate means to put them into practice. The sugar workers union alone, to cite one example, disposes of such a fund in the amount of half a billion dollars, and its insurance covers medical attention, sickness, and accidents during and out of work. The CTC, moreover, has taken up a place of full responsibility within the Cuban community as a whole, and at present develops its own economic program to compensate for the seasonal nature of employment and production in the sugar industry. Today, the Confederation counts

[9] *Living Conditions in Cuba*, p. 5.
[10] Confederacion de Trabajadores de Cuba or Cuban Confederation of Labor.

more than a million members—with its 500,000 sugar workers constituting the most powerful of the thirty-five national
federations affiliated with it and representing every branch
of industry and agriculture on the island. The Confederation
has drawn every fifth Cuban into its ranks, and has thus
obtained a much higher numerical degree of organization in
proportion to population than, for example, the much larger
movement in the United States." [11]

In short, the Cuban economy was making orderly, though
not spectacular, progress; Cuba was considerably better off
than Latin America as a whole; labor took a large and increasing share of the national income; the trade union organizations were large, powerful and rich.

On the eve of the civil war between Batistianos and Fidelistas, there were definite elements of weakness in the Cuban economy, but they were not those which would later be
adduced by the advocates of "agrarian reform." Specifically,
business profits were held down by the continuous wage
inflation, by injudicious laws which both hampered efficient
management and added to operating costs and by a graft-
ridden government which preyed on business enterprise.

The Economic Revolution

Since the Cuban economic revolution is in flux, all that
can profitably be discussed are the main lines and broad
strategies of development.

Obviously, the paramount purpose is to create a Communist economic system in Cuba as rapidly as conditions
permit. This presupposes the destruction of large-scale private enterprise and the economic liquidation of the rich,
the middle class and those professionals who cannot be
absorbed into the ruling apparatus. Economic liquidation

[11] Ernest Schwarz, "Some Observations on Labor Organization in the Caribbean" in *The Caribbean: its Economy,* edited by A. Curtis Wilgus, School of
Inter-American Studies, University of Florida Press, Gainesville, 1954, p. 167.

does not necessarily mean that these groups are to be physically destroyed or even necessarily imprisoned. It means that their economic power must be broken, because their self-interest, their traditions and their way of life make them inherently hostile to the process of communization. Moreover, this process presupposes the destruction of the business enterprises and free professions which keep them alive.

At the other end of the class spectrum, the workers and peasants are being bound to the regime by propaganda, indoctrination, terror and their incorporation into monolithic organizations which increasingly dominate their lives.

The revolutionary plan presupposes shattering the close economic relationships between Cuba and the United States. American business leaders in Cuba tried through 1959 and early 1960 to convince Castro that he was making a major blunder, that American enterprise was not reactionary, that it was interested in the welfare and prosperity of the Cuban people, that it would cooperate in any sound program of reform, etc.

This effort, needless to say, was entirely futile. It proceeded on the false assumption that Castro and his advisors were chiefly concerned with the material welfare of the Cuban people. Their real concern was with bringing or driving them to Communism, a process which would mean hunger, blood, pain and death on a vast scale.

The communization of Cuba presupposed the expropriation of existing American private investment, the creation of conditions under which no more investment of that sort would take place and the severance of the close ties that bind the Cuban economy to that of the mainland. This was necessary because the American sector of the Cuban economy was the hard core of the private enterprise system on the island. Moreover, the disparity in power between Cuba and the United States means, and has generally meant, both economic advantage and dependency. Having committed itself to communization, the Castro dictatorship was compelled to jettison its economic nexus with the United States and try to develop substitute economic ties with the Soviet bloc.

Obviously, this is proving and will prove a very difficult changeover. It is bringing poverty to the island and it will bring more poverty. The basic problem is that the American and Cuban economies are intermeshed by geographic propinquity, by complementary demand for each other's products and by the sugar subsidy which gave Cuba a preferential price position. The Soviet bloc is remote from Cuba in space, which means heavy shipping costs; it has not up to the present granted Cuba preferential treatment and it does not need Cuban sugar. Industry and construction in Cuba are geared to United States equipment and specifications. A switch to Soviet equipment will be difficult.

Moreover, the Soviet-bloc economic commitment to Cuba is based on political considerations. The Soviet Union is, of course, aware of the fact that the United States can bring about the overthrow of the Castro regime at will. Military intervention by the U.S.S.R. to defend the Castro regime would be as unrealistic and improbable as military intervention by the United States to defend Poland against Soviet invasion. If the Soviet bloc overcommits itself in Cuba, it risks, not merely loss of its economic stake, but a serious setback to its prestige as a world power. To the extent that the United States attitude toward the Castro dictatorship hardens into firm and irreconcilable hostility, the U.S.S.R. may find it advantageous to disassociate itself from a regime it cannot defend.

Engineers, agronomists, plant managers and technicians are being imported from the U.S.S.R., Czechoslovakia and even Red China. They are well trained, but few of them know anything about tropical agriculture.

During the transition years 1959-60, the INRA, an organizational monstrosity and economic super-state, made appalling blunders. Its thousands of rural cooperatives produced a bumper crop of tomatoes which could have been sold at premium prices in the United States during the winter of 1959-60. However, the INRA bureaucracy forgot to order crates. Egg marketing was taken over; a third of a million eggs were allowed to spoil in warehouses, and the egg czar was reportedly arrested as a saboteur. Cuban and American top sugar executives predicted a drop of at least 800,000 tons in sugar production under INRA management in 1961, bringing output down to a mere 5½ million tons. When INRA took over the fishing industry, various types of shellfish and seafood disappeared from Havana markets.[12]

By the spring of 1960, the Castro revolution had brought Cuba "chickenless Wednesdays;" pharmaceutical supplies were drying up; garages were unable to get spare parts, and dentists lacked gold and porcelain for fillings, burrs for drills, and anesthetics. As inventories became depleted, living costs rose 20% to 30%. An American economist in Havana commented:

"Terrific shortages of raw materials and replacement parts are developing which threaten the continued operation of many segments of the Cuban economy." [13]

The Castro regime emphasized a program of low-cost housing for workers. Under this, 10,000 units were built in 1959 and 20,000 were planned for 1960. The workers were to pay mortgages and become home-owners within 20 to 30 years. By mid-1960, the workers' housing projects, together with the other public works programs of the Castro regime, were at a standstill due chiefly to foreign exchange stringencies and a rapidly increasing dislocation of the entire Cuban economy.

Drastic declines in Cuban foreign trade forced the regime to impose strict exchange control, limiting imports to absolute essentials. Consequently, inventories of consumer goods, raw materials and replacement parts began to disappear as

[12] "Castro Farm Plan in 'Mess'," *Washington Post,* June 5, 1960.
[13] "Cuban Austerity" by Ed Cony, *Wall Street Journal,* March 27, 1960.

early as 1959, causing consumer hoarding, inflation and further breakdowns in production. The Cuban foreign exchange reserve was around $150 million in the summer of 1960, or about one-third of the holdings prior to the Castro revolution. However, the actual reserve in mid-1960 was close to zero since the commercial debt to exporters and others ranged between $100 and $150 million.[14]

In February 1960, Castro announced a 152 million peso industrial plan, a quarter of which would be financed by forced savings taken from the pay envelopes of Cuban labor.[15] The plan would concentrate on heavy industry: iron and steel plants, manganese and copper, chemicals, also textile plants and agricultural industries. Private foreign investments would be accepted only if "it is capital that is delivered to the nation so that the nation may invest it in industries of the nation . . ." [16] In other words, there would be no private foreign investment since it was inconceivable that businessmen would be interested in turning over funds to the Cuban dictator to spend as he pleased.

To competent observers, the industrialization plans seemed grandiose and impractical, involving the creation of totally uneconomic units such as a Cuban steel industry. Meanwhile, such basic economic problems as finding gainful occupations for the sugar workers during the dead season remained unsolved. In fact, the big strides taken toward agricultural diversification under previous Cuban governments were being negated. Rural Cuba, for instance, was eating its cattle herds in anticipation of further steps toward socialization.

[14] "Cuba's Trade Debt to U. S. Exporters Put at 100 Million," *New York Times*, June 9, 1960, p. 45.
[15] The peso and the dollar were equivalent until Castro took power. By mid-1960, the peso was worth about 50¢.
[16] R. Hart Phillips, "Foreign Capital Curbed by Castro," *New York Times*, February 26, 1960. Also see the Associated Press dispatch on the same subject and on the same date.

The Myth of Agrarian Reform

On paper, the Cuban agrarian reform law seemed reasonable. Landholdings were limited to 3,300 acres in cattle, rice and sugar; to 990 acres for other purposes. The owners were to be compensated in 20-year, 4½% bonds. Each land worker was to get a minimum of 66½ acres.

To quote a moderately sympathetic observer of the Cuban revolution, Theodore Draper:

"But Cuba's agrarian reform cannot be understood on paper. An INRA delegate, accompanied by a couple of armed soldiers, usually appears at a farm and announces that INRA is taking over everything but a certain portion. He may return later and cut the former owner's allotment in half. Though the law says nothing about farm machinery or cattle, they also are appropriated. The whole transaction is completely informal; there are no hearings, no inventories, no receipts. In some cases, if the owners are willing to accept INRA's offer, they may get paid in cash. No one has yet seen any bonds; the government says they are being printed." [17]

No Cuban peasant gets title to the land. "Except for one feature—the division of future 'profits' if any—the entire co-operative system might just as well be owned by INRA and the members of the co-operative considered as employees of the state." [18] Capital, machinery and fertilizer are provided by INRA: INRA markets the crop, and INRA pays the agriculturalists a wage. If INRA wants to announce profits and give the peasants a bonus, it can; if it does not want to do so, it can turn the surplus into investment. A Cuban Cabinet Minister told Draper that the government plans to shift over from these "cooperatives" to state farms.

[17] Theodore Draper, "The Runaway Revolution," *The Reporter*, May 12, 1960, p. 17.
[18] *Idem.*

In other words, the trend in Cuba seems to be toward communes of the Chinese Soviet type. There has been no agrarian reform in the sense of giving the rural worker land and independence. On the contrary, he was formerly free to work for anyone who needed field hands; he is moving today toward a state of affairs in which he must work for INRA at the place where he is wanted regardless of his personal wishes.

In March 1960, Antonio Nuñez Jiménez, the Communist geographer in charge of INRA, announced that 8.8 million acres had been expropriated and 2.65 million would be seized after the cane harvest. Thus 40% of Cuba's land area would be controlled by INRA by mid-1960 in some thousand-odd "cooperatives." In addition, INRA's bearded bureaucrats were operating "109 businesses valued at $235 million; 36 sugar mills out of a total of 161, 36 fishing and 6 frog cooperatives." [19] 1400 "people's stores," operated by INRA, sold at cut-rate prices. "INRA officials openly predict the People's Stores eventually will drive private stores out of business in the rural areas." [20]

Thus, socialization and expropriation were proceeding in Cuba at a tempo more reminiscent of the Chinese than of the Russian Revolution. Within a year of the seizure of power, Castro and his Communists were taking energetic steps toward the destruction of the *petit bourgeoisie* as an economic class through a comprehensive and frontal assault on independent rural retailers.

The INRA cooperatives are a Leviathan designed to keep the peasants and rural workers of Cuba in totalitarian, centrally directed communal organizations. Communal life will probably proceed, as in the Chinese case, toward the destruction of religion and the family. These "cooperatives" are heavily militarized and indoctrinated. They stifle, or are intended to stifle, any manifestations of discontent with the

[19] Draper, p. 18.
[20] Cal Brumley, "Cuba's Colossus," *Wall Street Journal,* February 24, 1960.

regime, any individuality of thought or conduct, anything which interrupts the lock-step unity imposed by the dictatorship.

As in China, there are signs that these coercive organizations will be swiftly extended to the urban areas, the population of which is more sophisticated, better informed and more resistant to regimentation. Simultaneously, public education is being reorganized so as to create a new generation totally indoctrinated in hatred of the United States, in the Communist *Weltanschauung* and in the concept of the beehive, rather than the family, as the basic cellular unit of society.

This is adumbrated in an article of great importance by Ruby Hart Phillips. She wrote about the new schools of Castro's Cuba:

"The pattern of training is similar to that used by many totalitarian governments. It includes indoctrination in schools, on radio and television and in the press; military training from 7 years of age; a hate campaign, this time directed against the United States; the organization of work brigades of boys from 14 to 18; and meetings and fiestas, all with a political purpose.

"The Government feels that once the youth of Cuba is indoctrinated with hatred toward the United States the relations between the two countries will be permanently damaged.

"The educational system has been radically changed in structure and purpose. Teachers are being instructed to instill in their students a desire to till the soil and work with their hands rather than become professionals. The teachers are also being taught methods to use in developing hatred of the United States and hero worship for Fidel Castro as the 'savior of Cuba' . . .

". . . All history books are being changed to conform with the attitude of the Dr. Castro officials, who have repeatedly declared the United States is 'Cuba's greatest enemy.'

"Among the changes to be made in the educational system, according to reports, will be the elimination of kindergartens. The 'specialty' teachers, who taught music, English, domestic science, manual training and other subjects have already been eliminated . . .

"It is planned, according to reports, *to have as many children over 5 years old as possible live at big scholastic centers, such as the one being established at Havana at the former Camp Columbia Army Headquarters. This is being done, it is said, so that the children will be under the influence of the teachers and not their families.*" [21]

What Are the Economic Prospects?

The short-range economic prospects for Cuba are continuing deterioration and impoverishment of the people. The reasons for this are multiple. Perhaps the most important is that we are witnessing the planned disintegration of a complex, well articulated economic system into something simpler, cruder and less productive. This revolution involves shattering the economic links between Cuba and the United States, destroying foreign investment, expropriating private enterprise and eliminating, through exile, imprisonment or death, the present trained scientific, managerial and technical personnel, since these elements are regarded as politically suspect.

This revolution is remorseless and irreversible (except, of course, by overthrow of the regime), since its basic purpose is to create a totalitarian society composed of regimented

[21] R. Hart Phillips, " 'Castro Freed Cuba from U.S.' Is 'Correct' Answer in Havana." *New York Times,* June 8, 1960. My emphasis—N.W.

collectives. In this sense, the Cuban Revolution parallels the Chinese. It is moving toward extremes of collectivism and State control of enterprise.

The fact that this involves simplification and impoverishment is implicitly recognized by Cuban authorities. The downgrading of educational standards and the stress on manual labor suggest psychic preparation for an era of economic deterioration.

Marxist economists and propagandists assert that Cuba's poverty is directly related to her concentration on sugar production and to the fact that a large part of the sugar industry was foreign-owned and foreign-operated. This is false. Cuban land is excellently suited to sugar production and there is no alternate way in which Cuba can acquire equivalent amounts of foreign exchange for industrialization and capital creation through agricultural effort. The dominant United States position in the sugar industry was of immense benefit to Cuba, since it meant massive investment in field and plant modernization, modern scientific research and business management from which Cuban enterprises learned and benefitted.

In another context, I wrote:

"The exports of these primary commodities are vital to Latin American industrialization because they provide the foreign exchange necessary for the capital goods imports with which new industries can be established. Underdeveloped countries which are attempting to develop modern industry always have an enormous demand for such imports. These must be paid for with foreign exchange and, in the Latin American case, most of the foreign exchange must be acquired with exports or long-term capital imports.

"Unfortunately, these plain economic facts are not clearly grasped by most Latin American intellectuals. Marxist-Leninist propaganda has spread the contrary view that 'colonial' and 'semi-colonial' countries are deliberately held in a state of backwardness as raw material producers by the so-called imperialist, exploiting nations." [22]

The brilliant British economist, Colin Clark, evolved the empirical economic law that the real per capita income of a nation tends to vary with the proportion of tertiary to secondary and of secondary to primary production. In other words, there are definite stages of economic development from primary production (chiefly agriculture) to secondary (chiefly manufacturing industry) to tertiary (chiefly, the production of services). A tertiary production economy is not one with a vast amount of unskilled domestic help; rather it is an economy which accentuates scientists, research men, management, specialists of all sorts, the professions, finance, communications, transportation, teaching, recreational services, merchandizing, advertising, etc. In short, it is a "brains" economy, in which a high proportion of the labor force manipulates ideas and people, whereas a small proportion is engaged in shaping or changing material objects.

It is precisely the tertiary sector of the Cuban economy that is being rapidly and ruthlessly destroyed. Before Fidel Castro, the problem of rural poverty was being solved. The solution was not to divide up the land, move out of specialized sugar agriculture into subsistence farming and thus both increase the peasant population and impoverish the country. On the contrary, the solution was the utilization of the foreign exchange accruing from sugar to develop industries and tertiary production, as a result of which Cuba was becoming urbanized. Rural poverty was decreasing simply because there was opportunity in the cities and the hidden unemployed of the agricultural areas were becoming townsmen.

It is a curious fact that the American advocates of "agrar-

---

[22] Nathaniel Weyl, *Latin America*, unpublished paper submitted to the Foreign Policy Research Institute, University of Pennsylvania, March 14, 1960, 72 pp.

ian reform" seldom consider the history of their own country. After the Civil War, the leader of the radical Republicans, Thaddeus Stevens, demanded that the emancipated slaves be given "forty acres and a mule," the land to be taken from the plantations of Confederates. Had this vengeful proposal been adopted, it would have destroyed the specialized agriculture of the South and reorganized it along Haitian lines.

When the American Negro finally began to make rapid economic gains, notably between 1945 and the present, he did so, not by acquiring subsistence farms, but by moving in droves off the farms and into the cities. This, rather than the Marxist-Leninist solution of "agrarian reform," is the normal method by which peasantries attain prosperity and progress.

Thus, the indications are that Cuba will pass through a period of economic regression and impoverishment. This is inherent in the nature of the contemporary revolution and constitutes the essence of its destructive phase.

This, however, is not necessarily the long-term prospect. If the Communist regime in Cuba prevails, it will use forced savings and other coercive methods to impose a very high rate of investment. Under these conditions—and particularly if massive Sino-Soviet economic support is forthcoming—the Cuban economy will display rapid national-income growth. Experience elsewhere in the world teaches us that Sino-Soviet propaganda is particularly adept at magnifying such economic achievements.

The United States would, under these circumstances, be compelled to adopt policies toward Latin America which would make it impossible for the Soviets to point to Red Cuba as proof of the economic superiority of Communism over capitalism. This presupposes a gigantic effort, affecting a continent and a half. It implies concentration on capital creation, which is the basic economic lack of the Latin American area. To attain solid results, the United States should concentrate its aid on countries which have strong middle classes, basically free-enterprise economies and traditions of due process of law and individual freedom.

Unhappily, the State Department has tended to move in an opposite direction. It is a national disgrace that the U.S. should have given bankrupt Bolivia $150 million between 1953 and 1960, or more non-military aid than any other Latin American country. Bolivia is misgoverned by socialist and Communist extremists, who have destroyed the regular army and substituted a workers' militia, who are hostile to the United States and who have managed to bankrupt their country, reducing the working class, whom they claim to represent, to appalling conditions of poverty and desperation. In eight years, to give only one example, labor productivity in Bolivia has fallen by 55%. Concentration of American funds in support of pseudo-socialist regimes serves no useful purpose if the regimes in question destroy the middle class and the fabric of the social order, thus making Communist revolution virtually inevitable.

13

What Is to Be Done?

> "The disruptive activities of
> the Cuban Government can
> no longer be dismissed as
> outbursts of inexperienced,
> youthful leaders swept by
> the upsurge of economic
> nationalism. They have all
> the earmarks of a well-
> planned strategy designed
> to make Cuba an advance
> outpost of the Soviet Un-
> ion's drive to infiltrate the
> New World."
>
> —Statement of the AFL-
> CIO Executive Council,
> May 4, 1960

IN AN interview with the publisher of the *Diario de Nueva York,* Spruille Braden, former Assistant Secretary of State for Latin America and ex-United States Ambassador to Cuba, gave an analysis of the Cuban situation which was in the sharpest possible contrast to the vacillating and appease-ment-oriented observations of his successors at Foggy Bottom. Braden declared:

"Cuba is completely in the hands of the Communists today. All its leaders are Communists. I affirm this without hesitation or qualification, and I defy anyone in government or out, to offer a single valid example of any policy or calculated act of the present Cuban regime which is not customary Communist practice and designed to forward Fidel Castro's and the Kremlin's plans for Red revolution throughout the Hemisphere.

"The tragedy of our State Department, and of our American foreign relations in general, is that we do not learn by experience. When the Communists began taking over in China, some so-called 'thinkers'—I prefer to call them 'unidentifiable THEYS'—in the State Department stoutly asserted that this wasn't really Communism, but agrarian reform. They argued it was a form of democracy, preferable to what Chiang Kai-shek offered the Chinese people, and involved no danger to us. Time, they averred, was on our side. We mistakenly thought time had been on our side when the Bolsheviks took over Russia . . .

"The fact is that today the Cuban Revolution is the spearhead of what Fidel Castro calls the 'Revolución Continental'. When he attacked the Moncada Barracks on July 26, 1953, giving that name to his revolution, he proclaimed that that would be the springboard from which he would take the Hemisphere . . .

"There is imminent danger that he will succeed, because, unlike the State Department, the Communists seem to profit from their errors. In Spain, and Guatemala, they learned they cannot win unless they liquidate the armed forces. Therefore, in Bolivia they obliterated the army and imposed their Communist government on the basis of a 'People's Militia'. In Cuba, even more quickly and dramatically, Castro put an end, by shootings, torture and otherwise, to the armed forces, so that he could entrench his revolution without interference from a responsible military institution.

"The same thing, unless adequate precautions are taken promptly, can happen in Venezuela and elsewhere . . .

"One only has to recognize the fact that no country has

ever rid itself of the Communist yoke without outside help. In Guatemala, perhaps the only country where a Communist regime has been thrown out, it was largely due to the vigorous military and financial support given by another Central American republic to the Guatemalan forces under Castillo Armas. The Red regime did not have time to get rid of the army—and the army finally threw out the Reds.

"Cuba, without an army, cannot rid itself of the Castro regime without outside help. Unfortunately, the United States actually has been helping Castro and the Communists with foreign aid, premium sugar prices, and otherwise. How stupid can we get? . . .

"There is now left to us only the possibility of giving assistance, or at least refraining from interfering with anti-Castro revolutionary movements which are both anti-Communist and anti-Batista. We are in the position of the man whose neighbor's house is on fire: if he does not help extinguish the blaze, his own home will fall victim to the conflagration.

"The Batista regime may have been a painful ulcer, but now Cuba is suffering from a cancer which, with indescribable agony, will kill."

The Caribbean as a Red Sea

By mid-1960, Cuba was governed by a dictatorship of the proletariat, guided by Moscow and Peiping. The only political party allowed to function was the Communist Party. All independent newspapers had been taken over; all broadcasting was in Government hands; it was a crime to criticize either the Castro dictatorship or Communism.

"All opposition to the Communist dictatorship, wherever it rises, is suppressed," *U. S. News & World Report* observed on June 20, 1960. "Secret police spy on the people, spreading fear. Thousands of political prisoners crowd jails." [1]

[1] "Communists Take Over 90 Miles from U.S.," pp. 62-8.

The danger which a Communist Cuba presents to the United States is many sided. From a military standpoint, there is the very concrete danger of Soviet-dominated rocket and missile bases practically on the United States frontier. In mid-1960, Soviet "geologists" were believed by United States intelligence agencies to be studying sites for submarine and missile bases on the island. The economic agreements concluded between Cuba and Czechoslovakia in June 1960 provided for Czech technical and financial aid in constructing jet airfields. Simultaneously, Soviet submarines were reportedly operating in Cuban waters. [2]

The most imminent military threat is directed, not at the United States, but at the Latin American Republics. The continent and a half to the south of us is currently in a situation of flux and acute social conflict, in which rapidly expanding populations, rampant inflation and other generators of social stress cause bitterness and discontent. These Latin nations are threatened simultaneously by internal Communist subversion and by military invasion from Cuba.

Cuba has become a haven and training center for Latin American leftwing expatriates. These refugees, augmented by international adventurers, Cuban soldiers, Caribbean Legion militants and, in some cases, common criminals,[3] are trained intensively in Cuba by veterans of the Sierra Maestra and of the Spanish Civil War. They reportedly also receive instruction from Soviet and Red Chinese experts.

Where invasions follow the strategy which Fidel Castro applied successfully in Cuba, the first stage of the operation is to gain a foothold in a remote and isolated part of the country to be conquered. Cloud forest jungle with access to the ocean is eminently desirable;[4] here inadequate communi-

[2] *Ibid*, p. 64.
[3] Reports were published in the Cuban emigré press in December 1959 that common criminals in the Isle of Pines prison camp were getting intensive military training.
[4] General Alberto Bayo, the Spanish Communist who trained Castro's forces, emphasized the great importance of seizing high ground in *Ciento Cincuenta Preguntas a un Guerrillero*, Habana, 1959, Año de Libertad.

cations prevent the regime from swiftly deploying well-armed combat forces to the threatened area and destroying the invaders. Once having gained a foothold, the small rebel force can receive supplies and materiel by submarine and rubber boats.

Once established, the guerrilla forces are served by the various Soviet underground apparatuses. Moreover, despite exchange stringencies, the Communist dictatorship in Cuba can make almost unlimited sums available to these invasion groups with which the latter can subvert governments and bribe hostile detachments to change sides.

Usually invasions are not attempted unless political conditions of disunity and demoralization already exist. There must be enough internal schism to create the reasonable expectation that a large part of the population and some of the armed forces will defect. "No revolution of the masses can triumph," Lenin wrote, "without the help of a portion of the armed forces that sustained the old regime." During the first 15 months of its existence, the Castro regime attempted invasions or fomented revolutions against the governments of Haiti, the Dominican Republic, Panama, Nicaragua and Paraguay.

The Latin American Military

Any realistic appraisal of the Communist threat to Latin America requires a positive approach toward the role of its armed forces. United States military assistance to the defense establishments of Latin nations threatened by Communist aggression should be unstinted and this may include provision of offensive materiel of war to these jeopardized states to enable them to answer invasion by counterinvasion. Certainly, any source of Communist infection in the Western Hemisphere can and should be placed in a position of decisive military inferiority.

This approach carries with it the danger that overblown

military establishments may be created, which will persist when they are no longer needed and burden the budgets of their countries. To avoid this, military equipment can be loaned in emergency situations much as staff officers are loaned. An alternate approach would be to establish regional defense systems, such as a Caribbean Group, which would be run by non-Communist member nations and would have arms of its own.

The attitude of the United States toward the Latin American military establishments should be conditioned by the fact that they are one of the strongest bulwarks against Communism in the area. These armies are becoming professional. During periods of social stress, they serve as forces for continuity and order. Over the last three decades, Latin American armies prevented bloodshed and possible chaos in periods when extremist right and left wing groups were armed and threatening to resort to force. "Had the armed forces remained neutral, or had they been unable to exercise effective control," wrote an anti-militaristic political scientist, "unruly civilian elements would probably have made Latin America even more unstable than it actually became." [5]

A Revived Monroe Doctrine?

The activities of the Inter-American Defense Board and the U.S. policy of military aid to Western Hemisphere nations are predicated on the assumption that Latin America "is threatened by Communist aggression both from within and from without." The United States has consistently refused to consider Communist subversion as an internal affair, but has defined it as a threat to the Hemisphere as a whole. Hence, American arms can properly be used to suppress Communist military and insurrectionary operations anywhere in the Latin American area. In the Cuban case,

[5] Edwin Lieuwen, *Arms and Politics in Latin America*, Praeger, Council on Foreign Relations, New York, 1960, p. 124.

failure by the State Department to recognize that the Castro movement was Communist-controlled, led to a withdrawal of arms aid from the Batista regime and consequently to the triumph of the insurgents.

After the Communist drive for power in Guatemala, Secretary of State Dulles worked energetically to replace the Monroe Doctrine by a collectively implemented cordon against Soviet aggression in the Americas. The Tenth Inter-American Conference, meeting in Caracas in 1954, resolved that "domination or control of . . . any American state by the international Communist movement" would be a threat to the Hemisphere sufficient to warrant "a meeting of consultation to consider the adoption of appropriate action in accordance with existing treaties."

During the first year and a half of Castro, the State Department tended to ignore this vitally important resolution. In essence, it transforms the Monroe Doctrine from its original purpose of containing European territorial expansion in the Americas (and specifically thwarting designs by the Holy Alliance powers to reimpose Spanish rule on the new republics). It gives the Monroe Doctrine the new primary objective of quarantining the Western Hemisphere against Communist regimes or Soviet control. This reinterpretation envisages the Monroe Doctrine, not as a unilateral fiat by the United States, but as a collective undertaking by the non-Communist nations of the Western Hemisphere to preserve the freedom of their continents.

Among other things, this approach presupposes that Latin America plays a very special role in the foreign policy and international strategy of the United States. A Soviet-dominated regime in Cuba is quite a different matter, in terms of United States national interests, from a comparable regime in Hungary or Tibet. In the world's present uneasy condition of both protracted conflict and precarious coexistence, it can be argued that there should be frank recognition that spheres of influence exist, that they are not inherently immoral and that they can contribute to the peace and stability of the earth.

This means working toward concerted programs by the Latin American regimes to minimize the political influence of Communists and Soviet agents in their countries. Inter-American cooperation is needed in intelligence, counter-intelligence and the general area of security. Western Hemisphere training institutions are probably needed where intelligence and counterintelligence agents can be thoroughly schooled in Communist strategy and tactics and in the organization and operation of the Soviet networks.

In the summer of 1960, a Foreign Ministers' Conference of the American States was finally held in San José, Costa Rica. It denounced Communist penetration of the Americas in general, but refused to brand the Castro regime or to recommend practical action. This was the logical consequence of weakness and appeasement, of previous whitewashing of the Castro dictatorship, of having reacted with gentle reason to gross insults and monstrous lies. Latin America was learning not only not to respect the United States, but actually to fear Red Cuba. The defeat at San José made the road ahead harder. It suggested that the U.S. might have to do alone things which it might much better have done in concert with the other American Republics.

The Cuban Case

Specific suggestions for dealing with the Cuban crisis would probably be out of date by the time this book went through the presses in view of the extreme fluidity of that situation. It would seem evident that the United States has enormous economic power which it can exert in this area, that the propinquity of Cuba offers unrivalled opportunities for blanketing the Cuban air waves with freedom stations located on U.S. soil and that the security problem presented by Soviet agents on Cuban passports must be a matter of hemispheric concern.

A revolution by the Cuban people against their Communist oppressors must be predicated on mass discontent and mass hatred. This is not automatically created by economic disasters and political injustice. It must be crystallized, channelized against the regime and directed from resentment to specific militant actions by a widely disseminated propaganda which is organized in terms of planned stages of revolutionary discontent. Thus, the radio is of key importance in the Cuban case. American-financed Cuban freedom stations can compete effectively with Castro's radio for the minds of the Cuban people. Should the Castro regime resort to jamming, counter-jamming would break the main nexus between the charisma of the Communist dictator and the masses who support him.

When it ceased apologizing for Castro, the State Department embraced the general line of "the revolution betrayed." This presupposed that the Castro movement originally had decent and constructive purposes, but that at some late stage it was taken over by Communist agents.

There are two major weaknesses to the "revolution betrayed" line in addition to its patent falsity. First, it implicitly accepts the Castro position that Cuban soldiers who refused to betray their government are "war criminals" and that Cubans who had enough prescience to oppose Castro from the outset as a Communist are reactionaries. It serves to limit the potential anti-Castro coalition to leftwingers.

In the second place, this approach reflects a much broader political fallacy—the doctrine that the United States in its foreign policy should seek to compete with Soviet-controlled groups in "liberalism," "progressivism," "leftism," or whatever it is to be called. In such a competition, the United States is condemned to defeat. The reason for this is that our advocacy of radical measures must be limited by our desire to preserve the existing social order and reform it by peaceful and evolutionary processes. The Soviets, by contrast, are able to support measures of an unlimitedly leftist character because their revolutionary program is divided sharply into two disparate stages: the violent destruction of the existing social order, then the construction of a new regime. In the first stage, wildly impractical radical measures are grist for the Red mill; in the second, completely authoritarian procedures are imposed to accomplish the task.

The "revolution betrayed" approach also serves to save face for those Americans, in the State Department and elsewhere, who through bad judgment or evil intentions brought tragedy to the Cuban people and diplomatic defeat to America. If future Communist consolidations of power in this Hemisphere are to be dealt with realistically and intelligently, it is desirable that the men chiefly responsible for the Cuban disgrace be eliminated from public office.

Democracy vs. Dictatorship

One of the reasons that American policy took the wrong turn in the Castro situation is that the State Department and most of American informed public opinion held a simplified view of the Latin American situation. It was assumed that *the* issue in Latin America was democracy vs. dictatorship. It was assumed that only the right-wing governments were dictatorships, thus completely overlooking virtually dictatorial systems of a leftist character which operated through nominally democratic institutions. It was assumed that the dictatorships invariably oppressed the people and were hated by them. It was assumed that the United States gave support to Latin American dictatorships, or, at the very least, failed to take measures to destroy them. It was assumed that the United States thus squandered much of the good will it had acquired during the era of the Good Neighbor policy.[6]

Some of these propositions are false and all of them are questionable. The demand that the United States actively support "democracies" against "dictatorships" is frequently voiced as a smokescreen by philo-Communist groups. The word "democracy" often assumes its Soviet connotations as in the so-called "people's democracies" and deluded American liberals find they are being inveigled into backing pro-Soviet, hate-America regimes which are considerably more savage, inhuman and totalitarian than the old-fashioned *caudillo* dictatorships that they supplant.

As of June 1960, rightwing, militaristic dictatorships were confined to two small, unimportant countries: Paraguay and the Dominican Republic. This suggested that the transition from dictatorship to democracy would be achieved gradually by the Latin American people as they advanced to greater economic, political and educational maturity, became urbanized, developed industries and attained national cohesion. The underdeveloped countries tended to remain largely dictatorial behind facades of democratic institutions which were seldom viable. Yet as an isolated and ignorant peasantry is displaced by an urban proletariat, as the landlord ruling class is supplanted by a capitalist one, the trend is toward more democratic institutions. If the changeover from dictatorship to democracy is caused by institutional processes of a fundamental character, the strength of which varies from country to country, it would seem rash for the United States to rush in and seek to complete the process.

The demand that the United States deny "bread and salt" to the dictatorships implies intervention in the internal

---

[6] An assiduous proponent of this view is Robert J. Alexander of Rutgers University. It is the central theme of his book *Communism in Latin America*, which has already been cited. In 1959 at least, Dr. Alexander excoriated the Trujillo dictatorship, but was unable to see that Fidel Castro was a despot.

affairs of Latin American nations to impose those forms of government which we have found suited to our own national character. The trend in U.S. policy has been away from such intervention since the first inauguration of President Franklin D. Roosevelt. The reasons for this abstention, quite aside from moral considerations, include realization of the fact that intervention generally brings the United States a harvest of hate and belief that the Latin American peoples will best attain political maturity if they are given responsibility and freedom to solve their own internal problems.

In recent years, most of the rightwing dictators have supported U.S. policies. In Central America, according to an intelligent and authoritative study by Martz, the dictatorships have tended to be more orderly, more constructive in the economic field and perhaps more popular than the real and pseudo democracies.[7]

The concept of democracy vs. dictatorship is objectionable because it reveals a narrow conception of American institutions and ideals. To the extent that we wish to transform Latin America in accordance with our own image, we should be concerned with individual freedom and due process of law at least as much as with democracy. In backward countries, these three institutional processes often do not move in parallel directions and the triumph of "democracy" may mean rule by a mindless majority, suppression of dissent, destruction of civil rights, flouting of due process, and oppression of the really creative and constructive members of the society.

Our broad purposes for Latin America would presumably include such other values as economic and political stability, the development of a strong middle class and of a free-enterprise economy, a system that is dynamic and expanding, that is moving into the full light of the modern world and not away from it.

[7] John D. Martz, *Central America*, University of North Carolina Press, Chapel Hill, 1959.

Reluctance to interfere in the internal affairs of Western Hemisphere Republics is a sound attitude provided it does not apply to situations in which one of these nations becomes an agency or outpost of international Communism. In that event, the United States and the other American Republics are bound both by the decisions of the Tenth Inter-American Conference and by their overriding continental interests to work to restore free institutions.

Time Is Not On Our Side

The political importance of Latin America to the United States is greater than its economic or strategic role. Latin America is the one great, underdeveloped region of continental proportions which has been massively exposed over a long time period to some of the basic concepts of U.S. civilization, to North American political and economic doctrines, methods of business enterprise and secular and scientific attitudes of mind. During the past century, there has been a considerable growth of hemispheric solidarity and a corresponding displacement of French and Iberian by North American cultural leadership.

Any serious breach in the wall of hemispheric solidarity must be a severe blow to United States prestige. Communist consolidation of power anywhere in Latin America will inevitably be interpreted as evidence that the United States is stumbling and that the Free World alliance is globally on the retreat.

In the last decade, three Communist-dominated governments have taken power in the Americas—those of Guatemala, British Guiana and Cuba. The Jagan regime in British Guiana was ousted by the British Government; the Guatemalan Communist regime of Arbenz was shattered by Latin American freedom fighters supported by a militant, courageous and dedicated American Secretary of State, the late John Foster Dulles. In the Cuban case, indecision and appeasement prevailed in the State Department during the year and a half which Fidel Castro needed to consolidate his power internally and create a proletarian dictatorship.

On December 1, 1959, the United Nations had 83 members. Of these, 20 were Latin American Republics. As the United Nations expands in membership through the admission of small, underdeveloped nations, the danger arises that many of them will be prone to take a pro-Soviet or neutralist position. Under these circumstances, any large Latin American defection to either bloc might leave the United States in a minority position. Since the U.N. is the visible symbol of world power and leadership, this would be disastrous. A state of affairs in which the United States could protect its vital interests only by exercising the veto or threatening to walk out would cast this country in the apparent role of a disrupter of international order.

Perhaps an even more serious consequence of effective Communist seizure of power in Latin America would be the impact on U.S. morale. In times of retreat, the forces of appeasement and subversion raise their heads. The mushrooming of fascist, pro-Nazi and peace-at-any-price mass movements in the United States during the years of German Nazi expansion provide an historic parallel.

Latin America can play a significant constructive role in Free World strategy during the coming decade. For this to occur, it is essential that steps be taken to prevent Communism from radiating outward from its Cuban base and to help the Cuban people to destroy the tyranny which is killing them swiftly and totally. The U.S. can provide leadership in the Latin American area, transforming it from a region of poverty and discontent into a stable, expanding area committed to the ideals of due process and individual freedom. Latin America can serve as a living example of the power of the United States to assist economically, socially and politically blighted areas to transform their institutions and to make orderly progress.

Index

About the Author

NATHANIEL WEYL knows Communism from practical experience and as an historian of subversive movements. While a Communist in the 1930's, Weyl not only was a member of the same unit as Alger Hiss, but also was involved in Latin American work and knew the top leaders of the Cuban Communist Party.

Born in New York City in 1910, Nathaniel Weyl was educated at Columbia University and the London School of Economics. He is a social scientist and economist as well as a writer. He knows Latin America from having lived and travelled there, from having analyzed its problems and served as Latin American research chief for the Board of Governors, Federal Reserve System.

His books include *The Reconquest of Mexico* (with Sylvia Weyl), *Treason, The Battle Against Disloyalty* and *The Negro in American Civilization.*